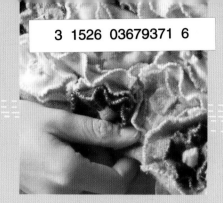

FABRiCATE

17 innovative sewing projects that make fabric the star

SUSAN WASINGER

INTERWEAVE
interweavebooks.com

Editor Katrina Loving

Design, illustrations, and photography Susan Wasinger

Interweave Press, LLC
201 East 4th Street
Loveland, CO 80537-5655 USA
interweavebooks.com

Printed and bound in China by Asia Pacific Offset.

Library of Congress Cataloging-in-Publication Data

Wasinger, Susan.
  Fabricate : 20 innovative sewing projects that make fabric the star / Susan
Wasinger, author.
     p. cm.
  Includes bibliographical references and index.
  ISBN 978-1-59668-094-4
  1. Textile crafts. 2. Needlework. I. Title.
  TT699.W38 2009
  746–dc22

                              2008039682

10 9 8 7 6 5 4 3 2 1

For my grandmother,

Elizabeth Mäder Abplanalp

whose hands had an uncanny power

to create, to teach, to comfort, and to inspire.

FABRiCATE

FOLLOWING THE THREAD

Sewing has been a part of my life since I was teeny tiny. My Swiss grandmother was a master seamstress, studying couture in Europe in the early 1920s. I used to watch her gnarled and freckled fingers nimbly summoning a fully three-dimensional shirt or dress from the flat, lifeless square of fabric. I was four when she let me sew my first garment, a pair of elastic waist pants in a green and orange floral. It's funny, I don't remember ever sewing a seam or a button before making those pants, but it would be just like my miraculously industrious grandmother to start me right in on something useful.

Could she have known what those tiny pants would do to my life? From that day forward, everything seemed makeable. I couldn't look at a garment in a store without imagining how it would look in a different color, or cut shorter, or made with a fuzzy fabric instead of a shiny one. This was of course both blessing and curse, leading to a serious and life-altering fabric addiction. But it was hard to find the "right" fabrics, ones that made me swoon and rush home to my machine with ideas bubbling and frothing in my imagination. Those big-box fabric stores were often a demoralizing ordeal where I found myself searching under overly bright fluorescent lights through endless cutesy calicos and novelty prints, and row after static-y row of variations on the theme of 100% polyester. Even the Internet, though dazzling in its possibilities, was a sticky wicket—forcing me to make my choice from tiny swatches flickering mirage-like on an inaccurate screen. By the time I finally found the fabric, often I was totally "over" the project. The search was draining off all my creative juices. It was time to fashion a sewing book where

the projects don't wait for you to **find the perfect fabric**, they begin when you have **made the fabric perfect**.

This book is full of recipes to turn humble and mundane fabrics into confectionery creations and visual feasts. It is all about the textures, colors, designs, and patterns that make fabric so beguiling and enchanting. So, stop chasing your inspiration all over town, sit down, relax, and start right where you are.

SUSAN WASINGER

NECESSITIES & SUNDRIES

I t doesn't take a vast arsenal of materials, notions, and glorious goos to get creative with fabrics, but a few, well-chosen supplies open up a world of possibility. Here are some of the essential ingredients that will exponentially expand the possibilities.

FABRICS The great thing about these projects is that they don't start with hard-to-find materials. Often, they start with simple, humble fabrics that are transformed into something extraordinary in the final project. Here are some tips on the fabrics I used.

Linens There is almost nothing better, in my mind, than a nubby natural linen. It has the amazing quality of appearing both elegant and down-to-earth at the same time. I especially love the natural flaxen/oatmeal color (see the Retro Messenger Bag on p. 98), but linen is great in a wide variety of hues, weights, and blends. I used lightweight earth tones on the Frayed Circle Curtain on p. 84, and a yummy mango-colored linen/cotton blend on the wave pleated Sundress on p. 26, all to very happy effect. Linen is thought to be pricey but is not much more expensive than a nice quality cotton, and it throws in its priceless character for free.

Cotton Cotton is the go-to fiber in sewing. It comes in a dizzying array of variations, is generally an easy-care fabric, and is extremely easy to work with. Most of the cottons used in this book are fabrics that are available anywhere. However, there are a couple of often-overlooked cottons that I think are worth calling to attention.

Osnaburg fabric is 100% cotton fabric with flecks of cotton seed, adding to the antique appeal of its unbleached surface. It is a less expensive option than linen, but one that will also add natural tactile character to a project (see the Pot Holders on p. 112). Look for it in the "utility section" of your big box fabric retailer, it's often tucked away on the shelf with other oft-overlooked wonders such as ticking, muslin, and that aluminized ironing board cover material.

Cotton duck is another great fabric you can find in an array of colors, often in that same utility section of the fabric store. It has a dense weave that gives the fabric a very useful heft and stiffness (See the Retro Messenger Bag, p. 98). It is durable and no-nonsense and adds a certain confident swagger to projects.

Cotton denim comes in a lot more colors than blue these days. All of them share that great mottled/heathered effect from the use of white threads for the weft (crosswise yarns). Our favorite pair of jeans has long taught us how beautifully cotton frays, and the Tumbled Frays Rug on p. 90 proves the point. If you are interested in eco-friendly fibers, check out some of the new denims that combine cotton with other fibers such as soy, bamboo, and hemp.

Felted Wool and Wool Felts Okay, I'll admit that this category of material might be my favorite at the moment, so I sprinkled a generous number of felt-y projects throughout this book.

The fuzzy woolen fabric used on the Ruffled Flower Evening Clutch (p. 14) was created by washing and drying old sweaters to create a feltlike material. The washing and drying causes the fiber to shrink into a tight mat, making the fabric thicker, furrier, and fray-free. It's a great way to recycle old moth-eaten sweaters, too.

The other kind of felt used lavishly in this book is the more old-fashioned craft-style felt, the kind that comes home with you in the third grade as a snowflake. However, it's definitely worth going a little out of your way to find a natural-fiber felt for these projects. You can get 100% wool felt (although the color choices can

be a little limited) or a wool/rayon blend, typically ranging from 20% wool/80% rayon, to 70% wool/30% rayon. The rich paint box of colors available make felt utterly irresistible.

I used to sneer at polyester felt, and yet I have included an entire project that uses poly felt (see the Shag Pillow on p. 32). This eco-felt, made from 100% recycled plastic water bottles, is actually quite good stuff—soft and lofty without a hint of shine or static. It's wonderfully politically correct pedigree makes it virtually perfect.

Silk As you probably know, silk is a made from fiber that is spun by silkworms. If you have ever seen one of their luminescent cocoons, you will be forever under its spell. One of my favorite weaves is douppioni silk, characterized by a pleasantly nubby texture, featuring threads—called slubs—that vary in diameter from fatter and thinner as they go along. It comes in a dizzying array of vibrant colors. Although it's true that silk can sometimes be a little fiddley to work with—being both slippery and yet prone to catching and snagging—it is also a wonderfully ravel-y fabric, which makes it perfect for cut-and-fray projects such as the Faux Chenille Wrap on p. 78. Silk comes in an array of weaves and weights, and the fiber has a naturally iridescent quality. Some silks heighten that radiance by using one color for the warp (lengthwise yarns) of the fabric and another for the weft (crosswise yarns). This creates a "sharkskin" effect that makes the fabric appear to be different colors when viewed from different angles (see the Crinkled Pleats Table Runner on p. 20).

Sheers If you want a translucent material to heighten an interesting peek-a-boo effect on your project, a sheer is your fabric. Sheers come in a variety of weaves, fibers, and weights. Here are a few of the most practical for the projects in this book.

Cotton voile is luscious stuff. It has a very natural feel, transmits light beautifully, and is easy to work with. While quite sheer, it is opaque enough to offer privacy and has a graceful drape, perfect for the Frayed Circles Curtain on p. 84.

Silk organza is very sheer but also firm, even a bit stiff. This makes it a good stable choice for use as a border in the Top with a Border on p. 60.

Silk chiffon is a glorious fabric that comes in delectable colors. It isn't the slightest bit stiff and falls in beautiful billows. Unfortunately, it can be a bit hard to work with because it is slippery and seems to be in constant motion. A simple project, with few seams is therefore perfect for this lovely stuff (see the Puffed Tufts Skirt on p. 38).

ADHESIVES, STABILIZERS Here are a few modern wonders that help to create all sorts of unusual effects:

Paper Backed Iron-On/Fusible Adhesive This material allows you to make laminates and overlays by fusing two or more fabrics together with a bond that is strong, permanent, and washable. Be sure to buy adhesives that are sewable so they won't gum up needles when stitched. They come in a variety of weights to work on fabrics from sheers to wool felt (look for brand names such as HeatnBond, Misty Fuse or Wonder Under).

Water-Soluble Stabilizer This miraculous stuff is most often used to stabilize machine embroidery, but I found a slightly less tame use for it. Sandwich just about anything between two sheets of this stabilizer (scraps of fabric, string, yarn, tufts of wool roving, lengths of ribbon), and it holds it in place while you sew together your inspired tangle. Once you are finished stitching, place the entire sandwich in water, and the stabilizer fabric dissolves away leaving your gossamer web behind. Check out the glorious and unique results in the Flying Swatches Lamp on p. 66 and the Swirling Freelace Placemat on p. 72.

TOOLS Of course there are the usual suspects that every self-respecting sewing box carries (see The Standard Sewing Kit below). But I have included a few extras that will help to make all your projects successful.

the standard SEWING KIT

You should always have these tools at hand before starting any of the projects in this book:

assorted needles for machine, handsewing, and embroidery

your favorite sewing machine

lots of pins and a pincushion

sharp scissors

iron and ironing board

Here are some other standard tools to have around:

straightedge measuring device of your choice

tape measure

craft scissors and maybe a rotary cutter and mat; for a lavishly practical kit, add thread snippers

seam ripper (though I'm sure you'll never need it)

nonpermanent fabric marking pen or pencil

thimble

Markers and pens Some modern craft wizards have invented the water-erasable marking pen to replace the tailor's chalk of old. They are available in color or in white for use on dark fabrics, and marks disappear miraculously when they come into contact with water. The "air-erasable" pens create marks that disappear in 2-10 days, or you can use the supplied eraser to make them go away.

Scissors and cutters In addition to very sharp fabric scissors and craft scissors, consider a rotary cutter (like the Olfa brand) for your tool kit. It's basically like a very sharp and accurate pizza cutter for fabric. It is great for precision, straight-line cutting for quilting, or laminated felt projects (see the Laminated Felt Laptop Sleeve on p. 52), or for cutting strips (see the Swirl Bag on p. 113). As with all cutting devices, care should be taken to keep all fingers and toes intact. The rotary cutters are a little harder to control than scissors, but they are indispensable in certain situations. You'll need to protect the surface you cut on. Cardboard or chipboard (the stuff cereal boxes are made of) will

work but might be bumpy and would need to be replaced often. Far better is a self-healing mat made for the purpose. It even has built-in measurement grids to make the task easier.

Straightedge This will give you a straight smooth edge to mark and cut against for many of the projects. Best is a ruler/straightedge combination, so you can measure and cut all in one. Metal or clear acrylic straightedge rulers 18-36" (45.5-91.5 cm) long are great, easy-to-use, and durable.

Measuring tape A measuring tape is always useful to have around, especially for measuring longer distances. Look for a retractable one that can measure at least 72" (183 cm).

Pressing tools I have two irons. One is pristine and has lots of steamy settings that I use to press garments. The other iron had a bad bout with some fusible web back in my early, overly enthusiastic days. Though I eventually got it cleaned up, it's the one I use when I am ironing on something that could goo up the works, such as iron-on adhesives or fused plastic (see the Fused

Plastic Tote on p. 46). It is my craft iron. Still, I don't want to end up with adhesive or melted plastic on it, so it's important to protect it like any other iron.

Baking parchment is useful for protecting your iron when working with fusible web. It is a thick tissue paper that has been treated with silicon to withstand hot-as-an-oven temperatures. I find this the best all-around material for hot-iron fusing. It is relatively inexpensive and very easy to work with; just tear off the right-sized sheet and go. As long as it isn't covered in adhesive, it can be re-used over and over again. Don't try substituting wax paper because it melts under heat and might fuse to your project or your iron, an obvious no-no.

For ironing your finished projects, a pressing cloth (modern ones are treated with Teflon) or just a nice-sized square of light cotton is very useful to protect delicate or embellished fabrics. Remember though, don't use a fabric pressing cloth with any adhesives or you may end up adhering little fuzzies and tufts to your project.

As with any ironing, take care not to burn yourself or any materials. Don't leave the iron in one place too long and check often to make sure that nothing is burning or discoloring.

Washing Machine and Dryer A couple of the projects in the book require a bit of rough handling by the washer and dryer. For the Faux Chenille Wrap on p. 78 and the Tumbled Frays Rug on p. 90, the more friction created by the washing and drying, the better the frayed edges will be. The same is true of the felted sweater strips used in the Ruffled Flower Evening Clutch on p. 14. After a pretty normal washing, I put the dryer on for a long tumble and added a Converse tennis shoe to give the fabric something to bump up against to roughen the experience. The canvas and rubber tennis shoe worked great, but I wouldn't recommend using a shoe made of hi-tech polymer-titanium-elestene (or whatever modern running shoes are made of); I just don't know how they would react to the heat of the dryer. Speaking of heat, for the Tumbled Frays Rug and Faux Chenille Wrap, I would suggest tumbling for a long time on low heat, since you aren't looking for any shrinkage, just fraying.

Sewing Machine Needles On a couple of the projects, a special-use needle will make your machine take on a whole new personality and allow you to sew beautifully with unusual materials. A denim/canvas needle is really great for dense, heavyweight fabrics where a regular needle might not be tough enough. This needle's shaft is stronger and its eye is narrower, for greater piercing power. A topstitching needle is great for machine embroidery. It has an extra large eye that is easier to thread and a deeper groove to keep thicker threads from shredding (see the Retro Messenger Bag on p. 98).

NOTIONS I can quite happily say that this book is a low-notions-usage zone. A small number of notions used in this book might need a word of explanation:

Extra-Wide Elastic This elastic band makes an easy-to-sew waistband for the Puffed Tufts Skirt on p. 38. It is available at most fabric stores in white and black.

Buckles, Buttons, and Snaps Fabric stores carry simple metal buckles (also called slides or sliders), but for faux tortoiseshell, leather, or wood (such as those used for the Retro Messenger Bag on p. 98), you may need to go to a specialty store or shop online. Stores that stock supplies for making handbags have a good selection of buckles, snaps, and closures. For the Laminated Felt Laptop Sleeve on p. 52, I tapped a wonderful, local high-end fabric store that has a gorgeous wall of buttons and snaps—each one unique enough to build an entire project around. There I found the ridiculously huge snaps that I used to close the laptop flap. Since then, I have found similar snaps made by a mainstream notions manufacturer (such as Dritz). Notions should be creative and fun. Don't shy away from the unusual or something you make yourself; it's the quickest way to make your project completely unique.

PART ONE

CRINKLES, PLEATS & TUFTS

ruffled FLOWERS

Is there anything more exuberant and beautiful than a bed of flowers in full bloom? Every inch of this fabric is covered in ruffled flowers made from strips of recycled wool sweaters. Making the flowers is fun and simple, a wonderfully optimistic project to work on in the dead of winter. For this project, the flower fabric is put to use in a deliciously chic evening clutch. This bewitching little accessory can give even the simplest frock its Cinderella moment.

materials

old wool sweaters for flowers

sewing thread

toolbox

handsewing needle

washing machine and dryer
(to "felt" sweaters)

ruffled flowers

To Start) Find old 100% wool sweaters at thrift stores or in the back of your own closet. Thin- to medium-weight sweaters make the best flowers. Machine wash the sweaters in hot, hot water, then dry in a hot dryer. This process should "felt" the wool, shrinking it into a dense, tight fiber that doesn't ravel or fray. Cut the sweaters into various strips, in widths of 2, 1, and ½" (5, 2.5, and 1.3 cm). The length of the strips varies depending on the thickness and softness of your sweater fabric. You'll need to experiment, but here are some approximate lengths that worked for me: 2" (5 cm) wide by about 8" (20.5 cm) long; 1" (2.5 cm) wide by 5 or 6" (12.5 or 15 cm) long; ½" (1.3 cm) wide by about 4" (10 cm) long.

1) Set your sewing machine to a loose zigzag stitch (p. 120). Zigzag one long edge of your wool strips stretching the fabric as you go. This will make the zigzag edge longer than the rest of the strip so it will ruffle to make a "lettuced" edge. I used the same color of thread for all the zigzagging, no matter the color of the fabric strip.

2) Starting with a 2" (5 cm) wide strip, handsew a running stitch (p. 121) along the unruffled long edge (opposite the zigzag stitching). Do not tie off.

3) Pull the thread tight to gather the wool strip into a circle.

4) Using the same thread and starting at the inside edge of the circle, sew the two short edges together with about a 1/8" (3 mm) seam allowance to complete the circular flower shape.

5) Repeat Steps 2–4 on a 1" (2.5 cm) wide wool strip to make a smaller circle; set aside. Tie a double overhand knot (p. 121) in the middle of a ½" (1.3 cm) strip (you will not be gathering this strip). This will become the center of the finished flower.

6) Stack the smaller circle on top of the larger one, lining up the center holes. Thread the two ends of the knotted center strip through both holes so that the knot sits in the middle, directly on top of the holes; pull tight so all three layers fit together snugly.

7) Handsew the center strip into place on the back side of the flower (7a). Push the needle through to the other side of the flower at the base of the center knot, then sew through the knot and stitch down again to the back side (7b). Repeat this until the center knot is securely holding all the pieces of the flower together. Trim the edges of the center strip if necessary. It's blooming beautiful!

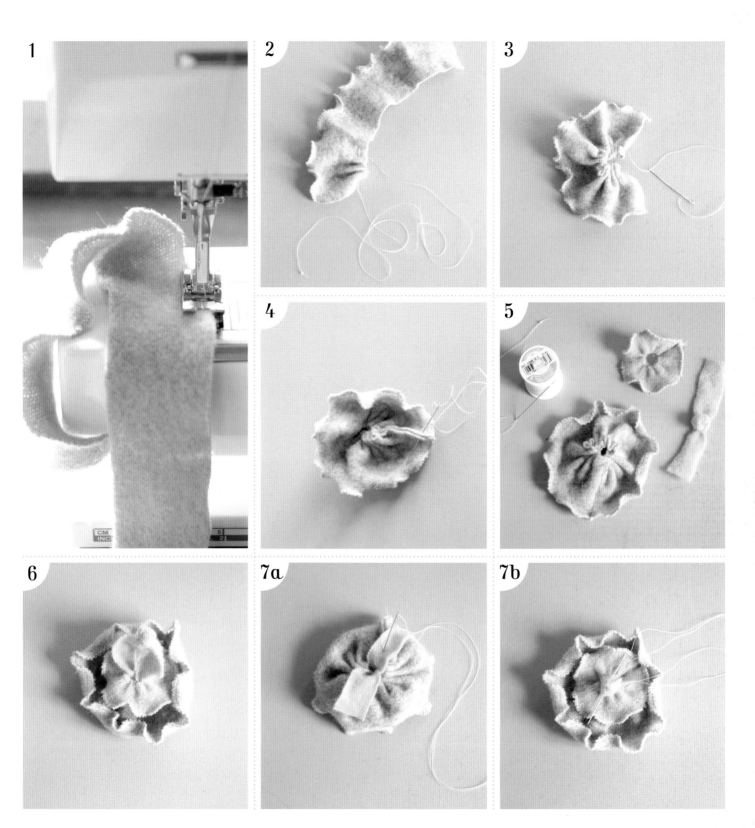

evening clutch

1

2

3

trim corner diagonally

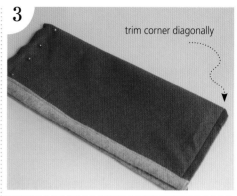

4

5

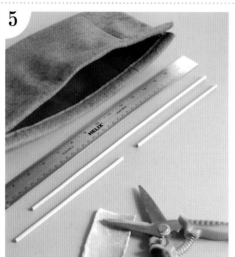

NOTE: Make two different sizes of flowers to cover your fabric: one bunch uses the 2" (5 cm) wide strips as its base. The smaller flowers use the 1" (2.5 cm) wide strips as a base and then are topped with a ½" (1.3 cm) ruffled layer and finished with a single knotted center.

6

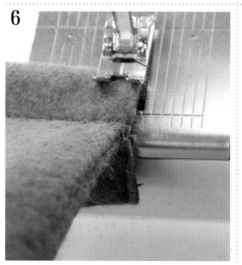

7

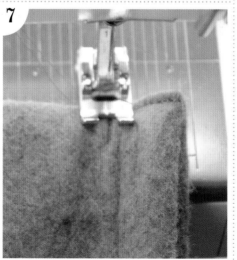

materials

4–8 old wool sweaters
for flowers

½ yd (46 cm) each of
100% wool felt in two colors
(I used green and plum)

sewing thread

36" (91.5 cm) length
of wooden dowel,
¼" (6 mm) in diameter

toolbox

In addition to the tools
listed on p. 16 you will need:

garden clippers
(to cut dowel)

sandpaper

finished size

6 x 12" (15 x 30.5 cm)

cut and stitch

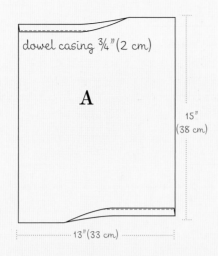

dowel casing ¾" (2 cm)

A

15"
(38 cm)

13" (33 cm)

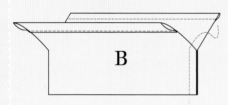

B

side seams ½" (1.3 cm)

evening clutch

1) Measure and mark a 13 x 15" (33 x 38 cm) rectangle on each color of felt (green for the outside, plum for the inside); cut out the rectangles. Trim the top and bottom (15" [38 cm]) edges of the plum felt, about ¼" (2 cm). This will create a smoother fold in the next step.

2) See diagram A at left for assistance. Lay the plum felt on top of the green felt, centering the plum felt so that the top and bottom trimmed edges are ¼" (6 mm) in from the edges of the green felt. Holding both layers together, form the casing for the handles by folding the top and bottom edges down ¾" (2 cm). Pin and machine stitch about ⅛" (3 mm) in from the edge.

3) Now fold the entire piece in half, right sides (p. 120) together. Pin and sew side seams, using a ½" (1.3 cm) seam allowance (see diagram B at left). Stop sewing just under the casings at the top of the clutch. To reduce bulk in the finished clutch, trim the bottom of the side seam at a 45-degree angle, as shown.

4) Trim about ¼" (6 mm) from the casings to make the dowel casing work gracefully in the finished product. Turn the clutch right side out.

5) Measure the top of your clutch end to end. Cut 2 dowel lengths, each ½" (1.3 mm) shorter than the measured length. Then cut one of the dowel lengths in half. This odd little notion will give your bag a bigger opening so it is easier to get at all the important goodies inside. Sand the ends of the dowels so they will slide easily into the casing without catching the fabric. Slip the full-length dowel into one casing and the two shorter pieces into the other.

6) Machine sew or handsew the ends of the dowel casings closed, about ⅛" (3 mm) from the edges.

7) Sew a short reinforcement seam at the top of each side seam (through both layers). Starting at the edge of the clutch and about ⅛" (3 mm) below the casing seam, stitch a line (about ½" [1.3 cm] long), parallel to the casing seam. This seam will keep you from putting too much stress on the side seams as you open and close your clutch.

To finish) Handsew the ruffled wool flowers onto the front side of the evening clutch (the side that has 2 dowels in the casing), covering every inch. Making sure to stitch through all layers of the flower, stitch around the center so that the flower is securely attached to the clutch but the edges are not tacked down; tie off. Take small stitches on the front of the flowers so that they are as hidden as possible. The thread should hide fairly well in the thick wool of the flowers.

You can cover every last millimeter of the clutch with flowers. Or, you can be a bit more demure and just embellish one side. Have leftover blooms? Make a brooch, top a chapeau, or add blooms to simple ballet flats to craft your own magic slippers.

crinkled
PLEATS

Here is a fabric that never just lies around flat. It moves, and undulates, and plays with the light and shadow almost like falling water. It started out simply enough, as a slightly iridescent silk, but a bit of folding, twisting, and a nice long tumble, and suddenly it's a material with a mind of its own.

Put it to work in a simple scarf or sew this lovely table runner that manages to be earthy and celestial at the same time.

materials

100% silk or rayon

matching sewing thread

toolbox

clothespins   dryer

old panty hose   microwave (optional)

rubber bands

NOTE: If you plan to create the table runner, skip to p. 24 for yardage requirements and cutting and seaming instructions before pleating the fabric according to the instructions below.

1

2

3

4

5

crinkled pleats

1) Wet fabric thoroughly. Lay it out flat, with the right side up and take hold of the top corners. Fold the fabric down about 1" (2.5 cm), then fold this pleat back on itself in the opposite direction. It's just like when you folded a paper fan in elementary school. Keep folding, forward and backward until you have worked your way across the fabric. Use clothespins to hold the pleats in place.

2) Now, team up with someone to hold one end of your fabric. Standing opposite each other, twist the fabric in opposite directions as tightly as possible.

3) As the rope of fabric gets tighter and tighter, it will begin to twist back on itself to create a two-ply twist. Keep twisting the now doubled-in-half fabric until it is ready to twist back on itself again.

4) Continue twisting the fabric, as in Step 3, until your fabric is totally twisted and resembles a hard little ball. Secure the fabric ball with lots of rubber bands running in different directions.

5) Cut the leg from an old pair of panty hose and stuff the rubber-banded ball into the toe. Knot it in place. Put it in the dryer with a few towels and let it tumble until completely dry. This could take a long time. If you grow weary of all this dryer time, let the bundle sit out overnight, in a warm, dry place.

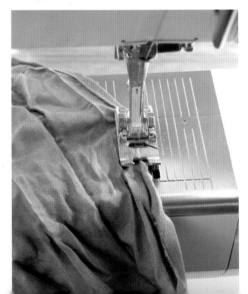

This intriguing fabric makes a beautiful accessory with very little effort. For a nice-sized scarf, cut the fabric into a rectangle measuring about 18 x 54" (45.5 x 137 cm) before pleating (pleats should run the long way of the fabric). Once the fabric is happily crinkled, just hem the edges to finish. To make a rolled hem, fold the edge in ⅛" (3 mm), then roll it over onto itself so that the raw edge is encased inside and machine sew (see photo at left). Hem all the way around the piece.

simple scarf

materials

1 yd (91.5 cm) of 100% silk or rayon
(I used dusty blue)

1½ yd (1.4 m) of cotton velveteen
(I used gray-blue)

1 yd (91.5 cm) iron-on stabilizer

matching sewing thread

toolbox

see toolbox on p. 22

finished size

14 x 72" (35.5 cm x 1.8 m)

NOTE: All seam allowances
are ½" (1.3 cm) unless
otherwise indicated.
Adjust cutting dimensions
for silk or rayon and velveteen fabric to fit your table,
if necessary.

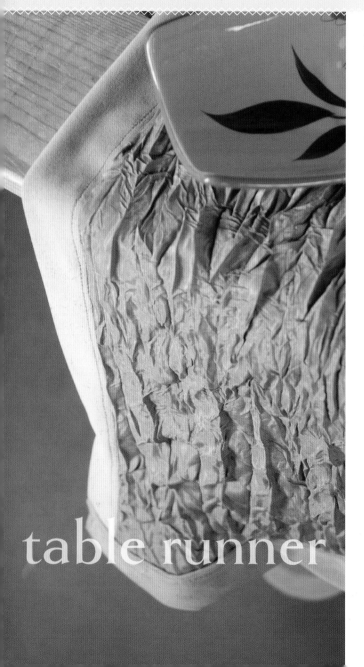

table runner

To start) Cut 2 rectangles, each measuring 21 x 36" (53.5 x 91.5 cm) out of the silk or rayon. Place the rectangles, right sides (p. 120) together and seam at one short edge to create a long rectangle measuring 21 x 71" (53.5 cm x 1.8 m). Follow the crinkled pleats technique on p. 22.

Cut a rectangle from the velveteen that measures 19 x 77" (48.5 cm x 1.9 m). Cut a piece of stabilizer that measures 11 x 69" (28 cm x 1.7 m). Following the manufacturer's instructions, iron the stabilizer to the wrong side of the silk or rayon. This will NOT iron out all the crinkles (you probably couldn't even if you wanted to). Trim away any overhanging silk.

1) Lay the silk or rayon on the velveteen with right sides together so that the long edges on one side are lined up and the silk or rayon is centered side to side on the velveteen (see diagram A above right). Pin and sew.

2) Now line up the bottom edges of the silk and velvet being sure to keep the silk or rayon centered. Pin and sew.

3) Flatten the "tube" of fabric. The velveteen will be wider than the silk or rayon, which will create borders on the sides of the table runner. Measure the borders and adjust until they are equal (they should each measure 2" [5 cm] from the seamline). Pin the borders right where they meet the silk or rayon (see diagram B, above right, for an end view).

4) Topstitch (p. 120) on the velveteen about 3/16" (5 mm) from the seam line.

5) To finish the ends, start by trimming ½" (1.3 cm) from the top sides only of the 2" (5 cm) folded borders at one end of the table runner. Cut the bottom velveteen at a diagonal, at each corner, as shown in the photo. Now fold the bottom piece under the top pieces of the folded borders making a neat corner and folding in the raw edges on the bottom piece all the way across. Pin to hold. Repeat entire step on opposite end of table runner.

6) Now fold each edge over another 2" (5 cm) toward the silk or rayon fabric to make the border equal with those along the sides of the runner. This will cover the raw edge of the silk. Pin and topstitch on the velveteen about 3/16" (5 mm) form the seamline. Stitch slowly and carefully over the thick parts. Iron the velveteen borders to make the corners crisp and the piece lie flat.

table runner

cut and stitch

A

fold
width
2"
(5 cm)

silk 11 x 69" (28 cm x 1.7 m)

velveteen 19 x 77" (48.5 cm x 1.9 m)

B

end view of runner construction

border
fold 2" (5 cm)

silk

velveteen

wave PLEATS

Here is a deceptively simple technique that can not only add charm and character to a plain piece of cloth but also shapes and sculpts a garment to flatter your curves. A series of shallow pin tucks (just another kind of pleats) is stitched down, first one way then another, creating alternating waves that will grace a silhouette with texture and movement. In this project, a simple tube of fabric is given all the shape and interest it needs with a couple dozen wave pleats.

materials

lighweight woven fabric to pleat

matching sewing thread

toolbox

fabric marking pen or pencil

clear, flat ruler

NOTE: If you plan to create the sundress, skip to p. 29 and follow the instructions through Step 3 before pleating the fabric according to the instructions at right.

wave pleats

1) With a fabric marking pen or pencil, draw lines for your pin tucks at 2" (5 cm) intervals and at the desired length (for the sundress you should start about 1" [2.5 cm] down from the top of the fabric, and the lines should be about 12½" [31.5 cm] long). These will be your fold lines.

2) Pinch fabric along these marked lines to create ¼" (6 mm) folds; pin to secure.

3) Machine stitch down the pin tucks ¼" (6 mm) from the folded edge to secure in place.

4) Starting about 1½" (3.8 cm) down from the top of the fabric, pin all the pin tucks down flat in one direction, then sew horizontally across the pin tucks in a straight line

5) Measure down another 1½" (3.8 cm) from the first line and pin each pin tuck down flat in the opposite direction. Sew horizontally across the pin tucks in a straight line, this time coming from the opposite direction from Step 4.

6) Repeat Step 5 to create rows of horizontal stitching down the pin tucks, pinning down the pin tucks in opposite directions at each interval. Leave the last 1–2" (2.5–5 cm) of the pin tucks free of horizontal stitching.

1
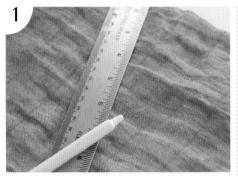

2
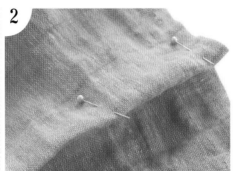

3

4

5
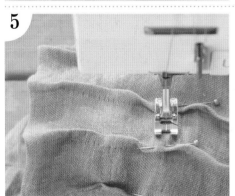

6

sundress

materials

1½ (1¾, 1¾, 2) yd (1.4 [1.6, 1.6, 1.8] m) of lightweight woven fabric (I used orange linen)

matching sewing thread

12" (30.5 cm) of
½" (1.3 cm) wide elastic

toolbox

In addition to the tools listed on p. 28,
you will need:

handsewing needle

pinking shears (optional)

finished size

XS (S, M, L) is sized to fit 28–30 (32–34, 36–38, 40–42)"
(71–76 (81.5–86.5, 91.5–96.5, 101.5–106.5 cm) bust circumference. All sizes are about 28½" (72 cm) long (not including straps). Adjust the width—yes, the width—measurement
(below) if a longer or shorter dress is desired.
Dress shown in size S.

sundress

This sundress is meant to have an easy, breezy fit that flatters the
shape without being tight or restricting. It achieves that without the
use of zippers or buttons, but to make it fit every body, a little customizing is necessary. Adjust the cutting template on p. 30 (diagram A) to
fit your size according to the following guide:

XS cut a 54" (137 cm) long x 36" (91.5 cm) wide rectangle

S cut a 58" (147.5 cm) long x 36" (91.5 cm) wide rectangle

M cut a 62" (157.5 cm) long x 36" (91.5 cm) wide rectangle

L cut a 66" (168 cm) long x 36" (91.5 cm) wide rectangle

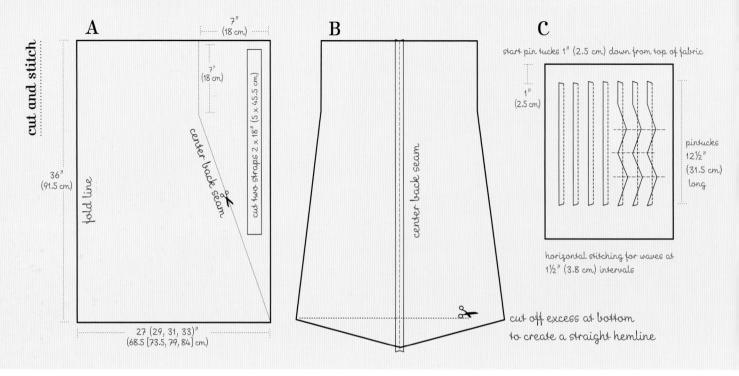

A

7" (18 cm)

7" (18 cm)

cut two straps 2 x 18" (5 x 45.5 cm)

center back seam

fold line

36" (91.5 cm)

27 (29, 31, 33)"
(68.5 [73.5, 79, 84] cm)

B

center back seam

C

start pin tucks 1" (2.5 cm) down from top of fabric

1" (2.5 cm)

pintucks 12½" (31.5 cm) long

horizontal stitching for waves at 1½" (3.8 cm) intervals

cut off excess at bottom to create a straight hemline

NOTE: All seam allowances are ½" (1.3 cm) unless otherwise indicated.

sundress {continued}

To start) Though this sundress is mostly just a "tube" of fabric, we give it a little help by cutting an A-line flare into the fabric. Start by folding the fabric in half widthwise, with right sides together. Then rotate the fabric 90 degrees so that you now have a piece measuring 36" (91.5 cm) long x 27 (29, 31, 33)" (68.5 [73.5, 79, 84] cm) wide (see diagram A above). Along the top edge, measure 7" (18 cm) over from the right edge and down 7" (10 cm); mark this point. Mark a straight line from the top edge of the fabric to this point, then mark a diagonal line from the point to the bottom right corner of the fabric as shown on diagram A. Cut through both layers along

the marked lines; be careful not to shift the fabric as you cut so that both layers are even. Using the fabric just removed, cut out the straps by marking a rectangle measuring 2 x 18" (5 x 45.5 cm) as shown in diagram A, then cutting through both layers for 2 straps; set aside.

The top 7" (18 cm) of the dress shape just cut out will be the "cuff" that folds to create the ruffled edge at the top of the dress. The cut line will become the center back seam of the dress.

1) Pin along the center back seam to secure by following the cut line (created above) and sew. Lay the dress flat as shown in diagram B, so that the center back seam is running directly down the middle. Mark a straight line across the bottom of the dress from corner to corner. Cut along this line to remove the excess fabric (see diagram B above) and create an even hem for the bottom of the dress. Backtack (stitch backward) for about ½" (1.3 cm) along the bottom of the center back seam (directly over the previous stitch line) to secure. Press open the seam and use a zigzag stitch (p. 120) or pinking shears to finish the

seam allowances (if your fabric is particularly thin, zigzag the seam allowances together rather than separately).

2) Fold the top edge of the dress down, toward the wrong side, ½" (1.3 cm); pin in place and stitch around the perimeter ¼" (6 mm) from the edge. Then fold this finished edge down, toward the wrong side, a little more than 3" (7.5 cm) to create a "cuff" and stitch around the perimeter, a little more than ¼" (6 mm) from the previous stitch line.

3) See diagram C above for assistance. Starting at the center front of the dress, make your first pin tuck according to the instructions on p. 28, beginning about 1" (2.5 cm) below the finished edge at the top of the dress (created in Step 2). Make 7 pin tucks on either side of this first one, wrapping them around to the back of the dress on each side for a total of 15 pin tucks. Measure the size of the bodice as you go to make sure the final measurement of the dress will fit you comfortably and flatter your figure. You can adjust the number of pin tucks for a tighter or looser fit. Each pin tuck tightens up the bodice by about ½"

(1.3 cm). You will need to add or eliminate them in sets of two (one on either side of the center pin tuck) to retain the symmetry around the dress. Remember that the back of the dress will be finished with elastic, so you want the bust measurement to have a little bit of ease because the elastic will tighten up the appropriate amount when you put on the dress, and you need enough room to be able to put the dress on over your head.

4) Fold the top "cuff" (created in Step 2) down toward the right side, about 1½" (3.8 cm). Tack the "cuff" to the dress at the edge of each pin tuck. Leave it unattached at the back of the dress for now.

5) Fold one of the straps in half lengthwise with wrong sides together and seam along the long edge and one short edge. Turn the strap through the open end, tuck the raw edges in ½" (1.3 cm) and handstitch closed using a slip stitch (p. 121). Press flat. Repeat entire step to create the second strap.

Place the first strap about 1" (2.5 cm) inside the dress and about 4" (10 cm) from the center front pin tuck and pin. Handsew the strap in place using a running stitch (p. 121), near the top edge of the dress. Make sure that the stitches do not go through the ruffle on the front of the dress, but instead are kept hidden between the ruffle and the front of the dress. Tack the strap down below the running stitch as necessary. Repeat entire step to attach the second strap, 4" (10 cm) from the opposite side of the center front pin tuck.

6) Sew a length of elastic on the inside of the cuff between the two last pin tucks on the back of the dress. The length of elastic will vary depending on dress size and the number of pin tucks used. Start with a piece about 12" (30.5 cm) long and use a zigzag stitch (p. 120), stretching the elastic as much as it will go as you stitch. Adjust the length of elastic used as necessary to fit your body. It is a good idea to try the dress on and measure the amount of fabric that needs to tighten up to fit you properly. Cut off the excess elastic when you are done. Tack the ruffle down over the elastic at intervals.

To finish) Try on the unhemmed dress and mark the desired finished length. Cut off any excess length allowing 1" (2.5 cm) for the double-turned hem. To create this simple hem, turn the raw edge under about ½" (1.3 cm) and finger press, then fold over another ½" (1.3 cm or as desired), press, and pin. Topstitch (p. 120) the hem about ¼" (6 mm) from the edge.

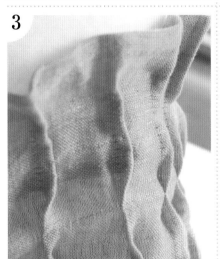
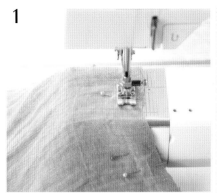
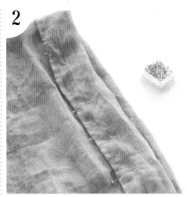
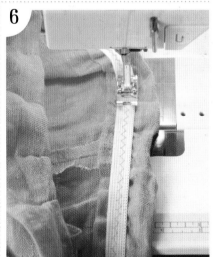
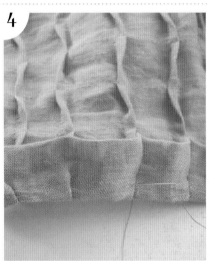
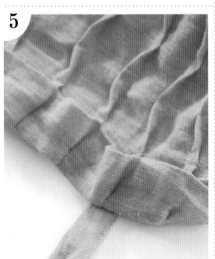

shaggy PLEATS

In the sixties, "shag" defined a whole attitude that managed somehow to be both rough, roguish, and refined all at the same time. And so this pillow, with its tousled texture, dares you to pass by without sneaking a quick touch. The deep, looped pile doesn't come without using up a fair bit of fabric, but this material has a secret: it is Eco-Felt, made from recycled plastic bottles. So relax; with every yard you use, you are keeping a lot of plastic out of the landfill.

materials

2⅝ yd (2.4 m) felt (at least 42" [106.5 cm] wide)
for the top fabric (I used cream)
(use either recycled fiber felt or a
wool or wool/rayon blend felt)
this yardage is sufficient for the Shag Pillow on p. 36

¾ yd (69 cm) of medium-weight cotton
fabric for backing
(this fabric won't show in final product)

sewing thread

toolbox

measuring tape

straightedge or ruler

nonpermanent fabric marking pen or pencil

cut and stitch

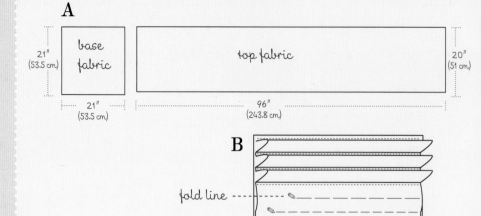

NOTES: If you find that you have run out of fabric before reaching the desired length of pleating, simply splice a new piece of top fabric by stitching it down in the bottom of a "trough" between two pleats so it doesn't show.

The cutting dimensions given here are for the Shag Pillow on p. 36; adjust them to your own project if you are not planning to create the Shag Pillow.

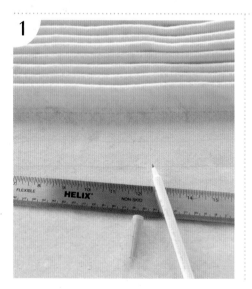

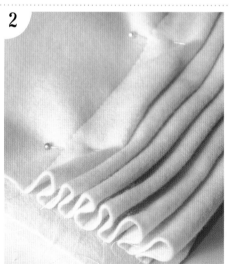

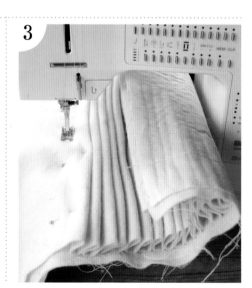

shaggy pleats

to begin) See diagram A at left for assistance. Cut two 21 x 21" (53.5 x 53.5 cm) squares, one each of felt and cotton (these will become the base fabric pieces); set aside. Cut a 96 x 20" (2.4 m x 51 cm) rectangle of felt (this will be the top fabric). Lay the cotton and felt base fabric pieces together, with the felt on top. Center one short edge of the felt top fabric on the base fabric so that the top fabric is about ½" (1.3 cm) from each edge of the base fabric. Topstitch (p. 120) through all layers along the short edge of the top fabric, about ¼" (6 mm) in from the edge.

1) Begin marking horizontal (widthwise) fold and stitch lines at 1¼" (3.2 cm) intervals, along the length of the top fabric (the lines will alternately indicate a fold and then a stitch line). It is best to mark and fold (see Step 2) the lines as you go (rather than marking the whole length before starting to fold) because it is easy to get off by a centimeter here and there. Those centimeters can add up quickly and it is easier to adjust, if necessary, as you go.

2) Starting at the first marked line, fold along the line and pin the pleat down to the base layers along the next marked line or "sew line." Stitch along the marked sew lines, sewing the pleat to the two base layers. Continue to fold the pleats, using every other marked line as a fold line, then pinning and sewing each pleat close to the base of the pleat that came before it (see diagram B at left). A good rule of thumb is that the base fold of each pleat should sit about ¼" (6 mm) below that of the preceding pleat.

 3) As the pleats pile up the project can get a little unwieldy. To ensure smooth stitching, roll the pleated fabric up under the arm of your sewing machine to keep it out of the way as you stitch.

Keep making pleats (I had 31 total) until you have worked your way down the entire length of the base fabric. When you reach the end, topstitch through all layers along the edge of the top fabric, about ¼" (6 mm) in from the edge.

If necessary, trim any excess from the top fabric. You should have a ½" (1.3 cm) border of backing fabric on all sides of the pleats; if you have any excess, trim this as well.

materials

felt pillow top (created on p. 35)

leftover felt from the pillow top for the pillow back

matching sewing thread

20 x 20" (51 x 51 cm) pillow insert

toolbox

See tools listed on p. 35

finished size

20 x 20" (51 x 51 cm)

cut and stitch

C

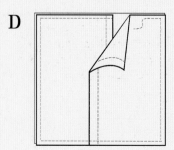

14"
(35.5 cm)

cut two of felt
for pillow back

21"
(53.5 cm)

D

Pillow cover comes off easily for washing.

shag
pillow

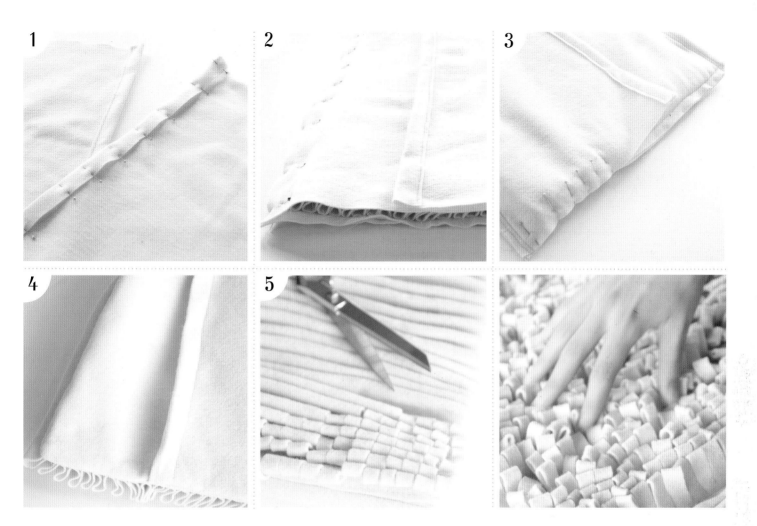

Shag Pillow {Use the piece created on p. 35 for the pillow top}

1) See diagram C at left for assistance. Cut two 21 x 14" (53.5 x 35.5 cm) rectangles of felt for the back of the pillow. Fold under a 1" (2.5 cm) hem on one long side of one of the rectangles and pin. Topstitch (p. 120) the hem about ⅞" (2.2 cm) from the edge. Repeat to hem the remaining rectangle.

2) Lay one of the back pieces on the pleated fabric, right sides (p. 120) together, so that the hemmed edge is toward the middle. Pin along the top and bottom (the short sides). Lay the other back panel over the pleated fabric, allowing the hemmed edges to overlap (see diagram D at left, this will allow the pillow insert to be tucked away snugly and invisibly). Pin along

the top and bottom and sew the seams using a ½" (1.3 cm) seam allowance.

3) Pin and sew the side seams using a ½" (1.3 cm) seam allowance. Clip all the corners by cutting a small triangle into the seam allowance at the corner, with the point of the triangle facing in toward the seam line. Be careful not to cut into the stitches.

4) Turn the pillow cover through the overlapping opening in the back. The pillow will be inserted through this opening when the cover is completed.

5) Using very sharp scissors, clip the pleats at ½" (1.3 cm) intervals along the length of the pleat. The pleat should be cut down to about ¼" (6 mm) above the stitch line in the trough of the pleat. Be very careful not to cut too deeply or nick the backing fabric. Keep clipping across all the pleats. When you have finished, tousle the pleats for a comfortably casual look, then insert your pillow and enjoy!

puffed TUFTS

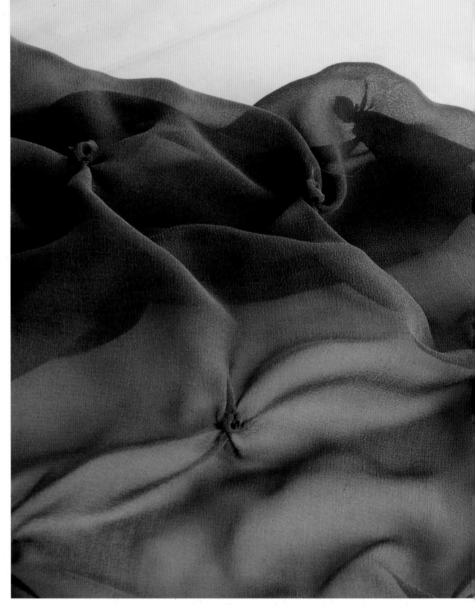

Oh my goodness! Who would have guessed that this heavenly confection could be so devilishly simple to make? The fabric is a diaphanous sheer silk that seems like it would need a lining to make it street legal. But folding the fabric in a clever way allows it to line itself with ease while gracefully highlighting the tiny tufts that make it so elegant and bewitching.

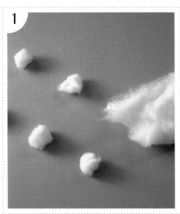

puffed tufts

1) Tiny pea-sized balls of cotton batting give extra fluff to these tufts. Tear off a small piece and gently roll it into a ball.

2) Tuck the cotton ball into the fabric and cinch the fabric around it with your fingers to make a "neck." Secure as follows: with needle and thread, start from the inside of the fabric to hide the knot and bring the needle through the "neck" to the outside. Wrap the thread tightly around the fabric, snug against the base of the ball 3 to 5 times. Then bring the needle back through the ball to the inside of the fabric and down through the neck on the inside of the fabric. Knot the thread twice, making sure the knots are snug against the ball, and trim.

These cottony puffs can add just the right gossamer touch to a simple sheer curtain. See p. 89 for instructions on making a curtain panel and use these tufts to embellish.

puffed tufts curtain

materials

1¾ (2, 2⅛) yd (1.6 [1.8, 1.9 m)
of 54" (137 cm) wide
100% silk chiffon (I used purple)

¾ (⅞, ⅞) yd (68.5 [80, 80] cm)
of 1½" (3.8 cm) wide black
waistband elastic

matching sewing thread

toolbox

In addition to the tools listed on p. 40
you will need:

measuring tape

finished size

S (M, L) fits 24–26"
(27–29, 30–32)"
(61–66 [68.5–73.5, 76–81.5] cm)
natural waist circumference. All sizes
are 37½" (94 cm) long including waistband. Skirt shown is size M.

cut and stitch

A

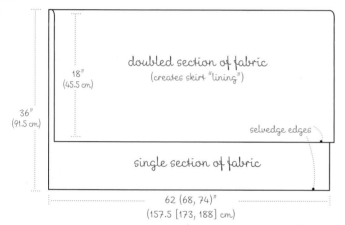

B

The tufts
should be 5–6"
(12.5–15 cm)
apart going
around the
skirt in three
rows.

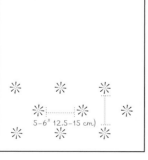

NOTE: If you would like a longer skirt, use a wider fabric (you can either use the
selvedges [p. 120] for the hem, as shown here, or cut to the desired length and use a
narrow rolled hem to finish). If you would like the skirt to be a little fuller, simply increase
the cut length by a few inches. You may want to do this if you are on the higher end of
one of the size ranges (e.g., a 26" [66 cm] small, instead of a 24" [61 cm] small).

simple skirt

Despite its elegance, this skirt
is simple to make. If you play
your cards right, there aren't
even any hems to make. Here's
how: Look for silk chiffon
that has selvedges (p. 120)
without writing or different
color threads running through
them. The way this skirt is
made takes advantage of these
finished edges to make the
hem for you.

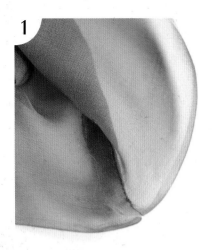

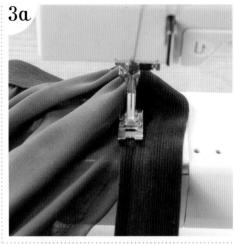

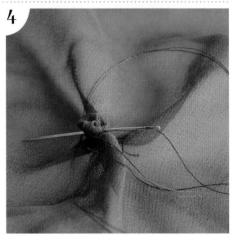

simple skirt

To start) See diagram A on p. 41 for assistance. Cut a 62 (68, 74)" (157.5 [173, 188] cm) long x 54" (137 cm) wide rectangle of silk chiffon, then turn the fabric so that the selvedge (p. 120) is facing you. Fold the fabric widthwise to create a partially overlapping piece that is now 36" (91.5 cm) long x 62 (68, 74)" (157.5 [173, 188] cm) wide, as shown in diagram A on p. 41. Baste (p. 120) along the top edge of the fold to hold it in place (you will use this basting stitch to help gather the waist in Step 3); do not tie off. Now fold this piece of fabric in half lengthwise with wrong sides (p. 120) together (you'll see why in the next step) so that you now have a piece measuring 36" (91.5 cm) long x 31 (34, 37)" (79 [86.5, 94] cm) wide. Line up the raw edges on the side, making sure that all of the edges from the first fold are lined up, and pin (this will be the center back seam).

1) Because silk chiffon is both sheer and prone to ravel, it is best to use a French seam (p. 120) for the back. Making one is quite easy: first sew a ¼" (6 mm) seam along the pinned edge (this seam is on the right side of the fabric since you folded it with wrong sides together). You now have a tube of fabric that is right side (p. 120) out but with an exposed center back seam.

2) Now, turn the skirt inside out. Fold the center back seam along the stitch line so that the raw edges are now inside the fold and pin along the length of the seam. Sew a ½" (1.3 cm) seam. This encases the raw edges inside the seam and finishes it on both the inside and outside of the skirt.

3) Measure around your natural waist with a measuring tape and cut a piece of elastic that is 2" (5 cm) shorter than your waist measurement. Using the basting stitch you made earlier, gather the top edge of the skirt loosely to help ease it onto the elastic. Turn the skirt right side out and, starting at the center back seam and ½" (1.3 cm) from the end of the elastic, pin the bottom edge of the elastic to the top edge of the skirt. Make sure the elastic overlaps the silk by about ½" (1.3 cm) (so that the silk is on the inside of the elastic).

Begin topstitching (p. 120) the elastic to the silk (3a), about ¼" (6 mm) from the bottom edge of the elastic (3a), stretching the elastic far as it will go as you sew and making sure you are easing the silk onto the elastic as evenly as possible. The more you pull it, the better the gathers will be on the finished skirt. Stitch all the

Skirt shown inside out here. The second layer lining should go to the inside of the skirt.

way around the skirt, overlapping the elastic about ½" (1.3 cm) at the back seam (make sure all the silk has been eased onto the elastic). Sew the elastic together vertically directly over the center back seam to continue the center back seam line through the elastic waistband (3b on p. 42 shows the outside of the top-stitched elastic, 3c on p. 42 shows how it looks on the inside).

4) For this skirt, I opted for smaller tufts with no cotton batting inside. Handsew the tufts into the bottom border of the skirt (single layer of silk) using the technique described on p. 40 and according to Step 5.

5) The tufts should be placed in 3 rows around the skirt, about 5–6" (12.5–15 cm) apart (see diagram B on p. 41). Measure, then mark the placement for each tuft with a pin to avoid drawing on the delicate fabric.

5

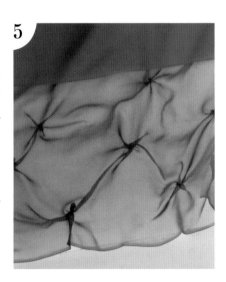

PART TWO

LAMINATES & MATRIX

fused
PLASTIC

Paper or plastic? Neither, thank you very much. Now the idea is to BYOB—bring your own bag—and avoid adding to our bulging landfills. But what to do with all those plastic bags that still find their way into our lives? Make this fabulously fused "fabric." Everything from old plastic grocery bags to the logo-covered bags from trendy clothing stores, even many dry-cleaning bags can be ironed together to make an interesting collaged material that is as tough and flexible as it is eco-friendly.

materials

plastic shopping bags of all colors and varieties; have plenty on hand with large expanses of white

toolbox

craft scissors

baking parchment

ruler/straightedge

fused fabric

1) Gather plastic bags and shopping totes. The bags can be a variety of thicknesses, even flimsy grocery bags and dry-cleaning sheaths can work. However, biodegradable plastics are NOT a good choice. If in doubt, test a sample to see if the plastic melts and bonds well with others by following the technique described in Step 3.

2) Cut off handles and open side and/or bottom seams to get the largest flat piece of plastic from each bag. Logos and words will show through in the final "collage," use or avoid them as you prefer. For my fabrics, I like to use some words and logos, but I make sure they are covered with a few layers of white plastic to make them more subdued.

3) Lay down a piece of baking parchment to protect your ironing surface. Stack together about 5 layers of plastic. It is fine to piece together lots of smaller sections to make a larger piece; just be sure to overlap everything by a couple of inches. Cover the stack of plastic with another piece of baking parchment and iron on a hot setting (no steam). The fabric will shrink a bit as it melts. Go over the whole area 2 or 3 times, letting the iron linger for 3–5 seconds on each section as you go. Let the fabric cool (the baking parchment will signal the cooling by noisily starting to pull off of the plastic fabric).

4) Turn the fabric and baking parchment "sandwich" over and iron on the other side as before. Check to see that the fabric is truly fusing together into one material. If not, continue ironing, lingering a little longer on each section. Add more layers if you want thicker fabric. This fabric can overlap and fuse together with others to make larger pieces of fabric.

1

2

3

4
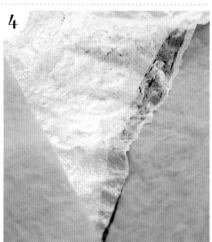

Add decorative elements to your top surface by ironing on circles, stripes, or collaging together small illustrations like the "flower" seen at far right. Different plastic materials and colors melt differently and shrink at different rates, so always test with a small piece first to see how it works.

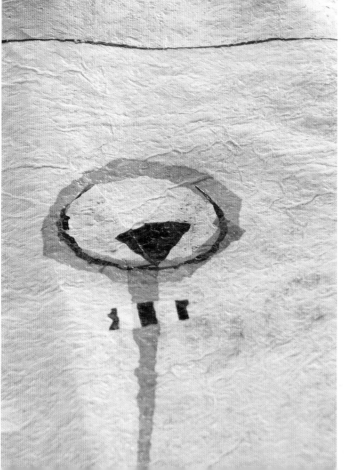

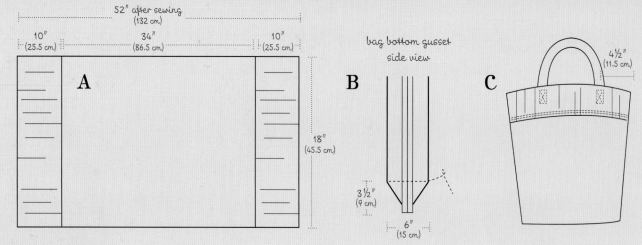

52" after sewing
(132 cm)

10"
(25.5 cm)

34"
(86.5 cm)

10"
(25.5 cm)

A

18"
(45.5 cm)

*bag bottom gusset
side view*

B

3½"
(9 cm)

6"
(15 cm)

C

4½"
(11.5 cm)

materials

10–20 plastic shopping bags of all colors and varieties; have plenty on hand with large expanses of white

toolbox

See tools listed on p. 48

finished size

19" (48.5 cm) tall x 17" (43 cm) wide x 6" (15 cm) deep

recycled plastic tote

To start) According to the instructions on p. 48, create 1 rectangle of predominantly white fused plastic fabric that can be trimmed to measure 18 x 34" (45.5 x 86.5 cm). Additionally, make two more sections of fused plastic fabric that can each be trimmed to 18 x 10" (45.5 x 26.5 cm). You'll also need a piece of green or blue plastic fabric about 23 x 3 " (58.5 x 7.5 cm), which you can cut in half to create two 1½" (3.8 cm) wide straps.

1) Add vertical stripes of blues, greens, and grays to 2 smaller 18 x 10" (45.5 x 26.5 cm) rectangles. Trim excess if necessary to maintain the original measurements.

2) Lay one of the striped bands (created in Step 1) on one side of the white 18 x 34" (45.5 x 86.5 cm) rectangle, right sides together. Match up the edges and pin. Repeat with the remaining striped band on the other end of the white rectangle, then sew the striped bands of fabric to the white rectangle, making a long rectangle with striped borders (see diagram A above). This new piece should measure 18 x 52" (45.5 x 132 cm).

3) Fold this long rectangle in half with right sides (p. 120) together, so that the striped bands are lying together (the striped bands are at the top of the bag).

4) Pin and then sew the side seams.

5) Make the bottom gussets (p. 120) to give the bag shape, as follows: lay the bag flat so that the side seam is facing you, and running down the middle of the bag (see diagram B above).

Measure 3½" (9 cm) up from the bottom corner of the side seam and mark, then mark a line across the width (edge to edge). This line will be about 6" (15 cm) long. Sew a seam across this line. Repeat entire step on the other side of the bag to create the second gusset.

6) Turn the bag right side out. Note how the gusset forms a stable bottom for the bag. Now fold the top striped fabric in half, down into the bag to form a double border along the bag's top edge. The border fabric should reach far enough down into the bag's interior to cover the seam formed in Step 2.

7) Pin the border fabric down and topstitch (p. 120) on the border around the perimeter of the bag, about ⅛" (3 mm) from the edge.

8) Fold the long edges of 1 strap in about ¼" (6 mm), then fold the strap in half to make a double-layer strap that is about 1" (2.5 cm) wide and pin. Topstitch the strap together, about ⅛" (3 mm) from the edge. Topstitch along the other long edge, about ⅛" (3 mm) from the edge to make a neat strap with stitching on both sides.

9) See diagram C above for assistance. Mark the 4 spots on the bag border where the straps will be attached (2 on each side). Each mark should be 4½" (11.5 cm) over from the side seam. Place the ends of 1 strap about 2¼" (5.5 cm) into the bag's interior at the marks as shown in diagram C, placing them just over the marks to hide them. Sew the ends of the strap to the bag using a box stitch with an X in the middle to hold the strap securely, as shown. Repeat entire step to attach the remaining strap to the other side of the bag.

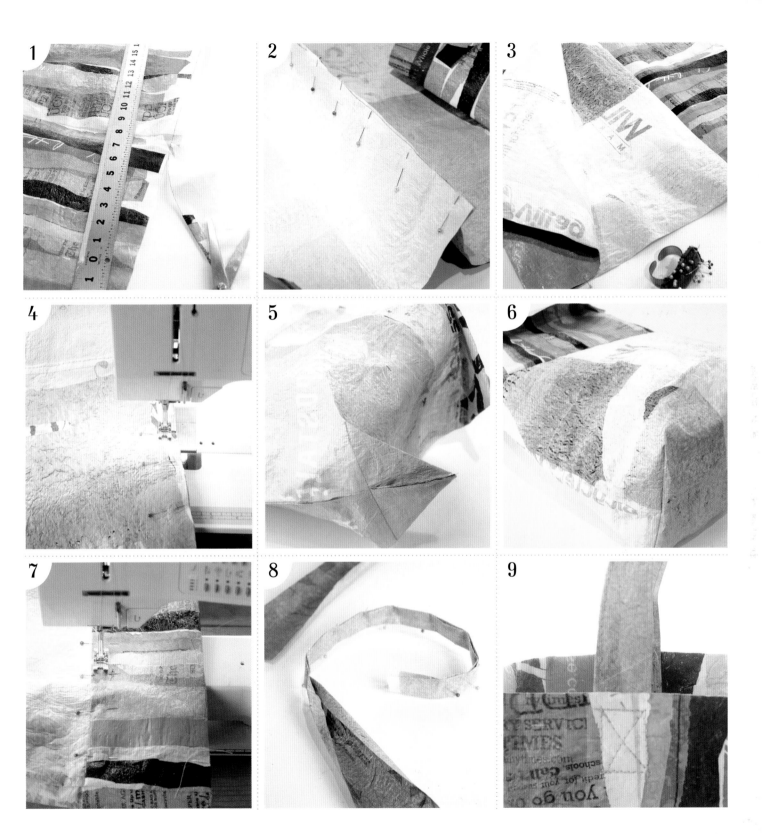

laminated FELT

Usually, it is the front rather than the side view of a fabric that makes it swoon-worthy. But this laminated felt fabric has strata of color that makes it interesting from all angles. The thick, cushioning fabric is perfect for making a portfolio, a notebook cover, or a laptop sleeve like the one seen here. The fabric is firm enough to provide structural integrity, yet soft enough to baby your computer. You can make it your own by customizing colors and adding handles, snaps, or even a laminated-felt button.

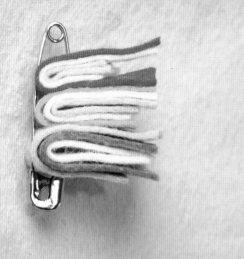

materials

1¼ yd (1.1 m) of 100% wool or wool/rayon blend felt in 3 to 4 colors (I used sky blue, red, cream, and gold)

iron-on adhesive (be sure it is sewable adhesive so it doesn't gum up needles)

toolbox

iron

baking parchment

scissors or rotary cutter and self-healing cutting mat

ruler/straightedge

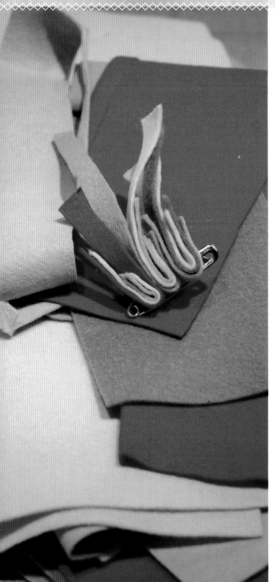

laminated felt

To start) Play with color combinations for your laminated fabric. Make laminated felt pieces oversized so you can trim back to your finished size and expose the stratified edge.

1) Cut felt and iron-on adhesive to larger than finished size (see note on p. 56). Place a piece of the cut iron-on adhesive between 2 of the felt pieces and then sandwich all 3 layers between 2 pieces of baking parchment to protect your ironing surface and iron. Following manufacturer's instructions, fuse these first 2 pieces of felt together.

2) Add the next color of felt to your stack and fuse as before. Repeat with one or two more layers to make a thick, stiff yet still pliable fabric.

1

2

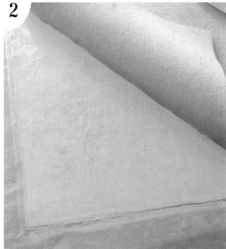

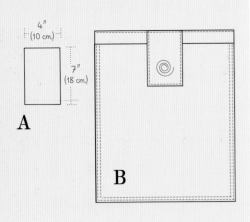

4"
(10 cm)

7"
(18 cm)

A

B

length plus 3½" (9 cm)

width plus 3½" (9cm)

Laptop sizes vary so you'll need to measure your own laptop before beginning. The best rule of thumb is to take the laptop measurements (length and width) and add 3½" (9 cm) to each. This gives you an extra 2" (5 cm) to fit the thickness of the laptop, and 1½" (3.8 cm) to account for seams and final trim. My computer measures 14 x 9½" (35.5 x 24 cm), so I cut my pieces to be 17½ x 13" (44.5 x 33 cm) to start.

materials

lamintated felt from p. 55

matching sewing thread

oversized snap (I used a 1" [2.5 cm] snap)

toolbox

in addition to the tools listed on p. 55 you will need:

handsewing needle

thimble (optional)

laptop sleeve

To start) Determine the measurements of the felt pieces appropriate for your laptop. Make pieces of layered felt large enough to cut out the pieces for your laptop sleeve. For my laptop sleeve, I used one layer each of sky blue, red, cream, and then gold.

1) Once the felt is layered, cut out the 2 large rectangles for the front and back of the sleeve. Be sure to cut through all layers. Cut 1 laminated rectangle 1" (2.5 cm) shorter than the other, the shorter rectangle will become the front of the laptop sleeve. You can use very sharp scissors and a steady hand to cut the rectangles, but for clean, straight cuts that show maximum stratification, a rotary cutter works great. You will have

to use firm pressure and several passes with the cutter to get through all the layers.

Cut one more rectangle out of the laminated felt, measuring 7 x 4" (18 x 10 cm) for the tab closure (see diagram A at top left).

2) See diagram B at top left for assistance. Lay the shorter front piece together with the back piece, with wrong sides (p. 120) together so that the side and bottom edges match up (the top edge of the front will be 1" [2.5 cm] lower than the back). Topstitch (p. 120) the front of the sleeve to the back along the sides and bottom, using a ½" (1.3 cm) seam allowance, and turning at the corners to create a continuous stitch line.

1

2

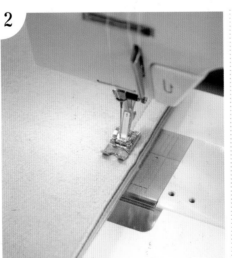

3

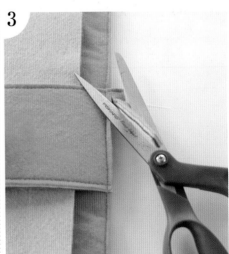

Topstitch (p. 120) a second line of stitching ¼" (6 mm) in from the first. Using scissors or a rotary cutter, trim the seams back to about ⅛" (3 mm) from the outer stitch line.

3) For the tab closure, topstitch around the outside edge of the tab on three sides, about ⅛" (3 mm) from the edge, leaving the top edge (one short edge) free of stitching. Center the tab on the laptop sleeve, letting the tab overhang the top edge of the back by about ¼" (6 mm). Topstitch across the top of the laptop sleeve, about ⅛" (3 mm) from the top edge of the laptop sleeve, stitching right over the tab as you go. Trim the excess material from the top of the tab so it is even with the laptop sleeve's top edge.

4) Measure up about 1½" (3.8 cm) from the bottom of the tab closure and mark. Center the button (see p. 58 for instructions on making the spiral button) on the tab closure, placing the bottom edge of the button just over the mark to hide it. Stitch the button in place with a slip stitch (p. 121), being sure to take the stitches under the button so that they are hidden.

Center the male snap on the wrong side (p. 120) of the tab, directly under the button (about 2" [5 cm] from the end). Whipstitch (p. 121) in place with doubled thread. Mark the corresponding place on the laptop sleeve where you will want the female snap; place the snap and be sure to check that the two sides of the snap match up when closed. Whipstitch the female snap in place as before.

4

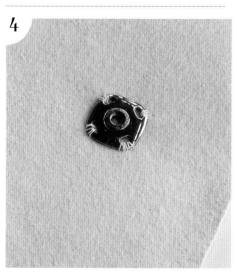

laptop sleeve

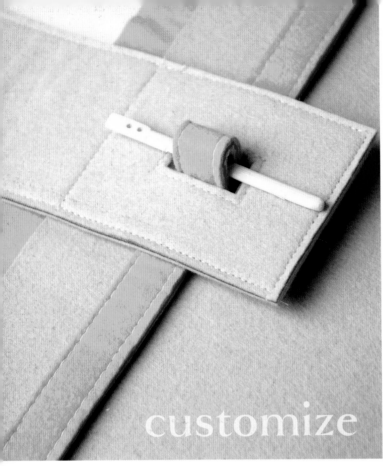

customize

hasp and pin This is a fancy and elegant notion that has been used throughout history to close everything from purses to castle gates. For this version, a narrow strap of felt sticks up to make a loop through a sewn square hole in the tab. Any narrow object would work for the pin, a pencil or favorite pen could be nice and you would have a built-in pen loop. Here, I customized a fast-food chopstick by cutting it short, sanding it smooth, and drilling two tiny holes in it so it can be attached to the laptop sleeve permanently with string or yarn.

spiral button I love this homemade button! To make the spiral button, cut a long, narrow strip of the same laminated felt used for the laptop sleeve (mine was about 12 x ½" [30.5 x 1.3 cm], but you can adjust according to the size of button you would like). Zigzag (p. 120) down the middle of the strip; this will help to hold it together through all the tight turns. Starting at one end, roll the strip in a spiral, stitching through the layers with a needle and doubled thread as you go to secure. A thimble really comes in handy here because the needle needs some extra push to get through the layers (alternatively, you could use a pair of needle-nose pliers to pull the needle through when the going gets rough). Just make sure each subsequent layer of the spiral is well-attached to the layers before it.

snaps There are some really interesting and practical snaps and closers currently available. These mechanical, male/female snaps are just oversized versions of the ones that were ubiquitous before Velcro was invented. They work well and have a sort of super-sized charm. Another possible closer is a magnetic purse snap. It uses a strong magnetic attraction to do the job. It attaches easily and has a satisfying sound when it closes (see resources on p. 124).

handles You can add a handle to your laptop sleeve or portfolio and really show off the striped dimension of the laminated fabric, as well as making the sleeve or portfolio convenient to throw over you shoulder. Cut a strip of laminated felt and topstitch (p. 120) along both sides, about ⅛" (3 mm) from the edge. The handle can attach easily to the inside of the laptop sleeve with a line or two of stitching or a stitched box with an "X" through it (see the Step 9 photo on p. 51).

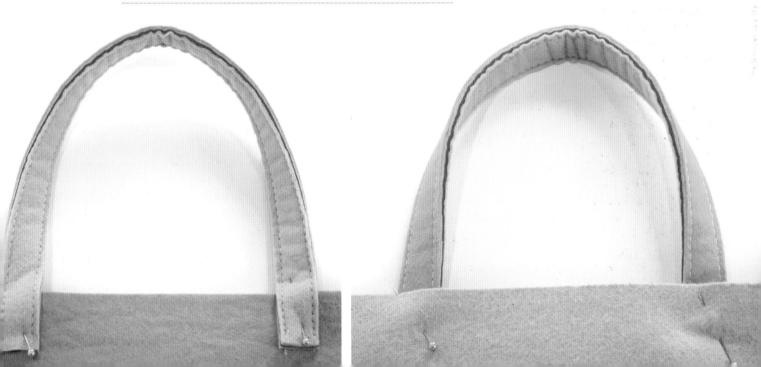

stitchless EMBROIDERY

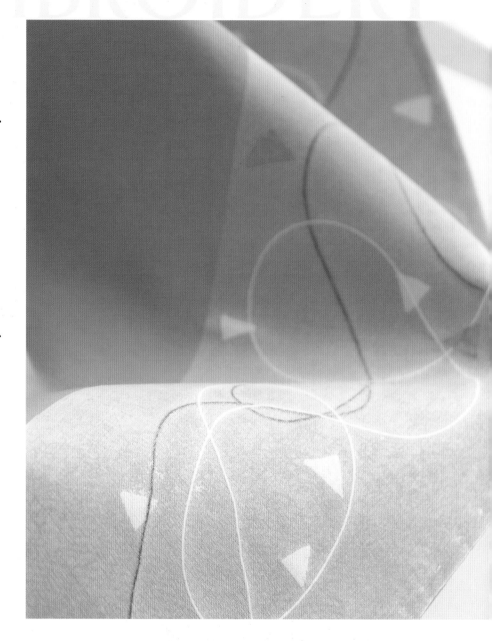

It seems slightly scandalous that you can "embroider" a beguiling little motif onto fabric without knowing a thing about needlecraft or sewing a single stitch. However, in a process more akin to collage than sewing, snips of color and meandering loops of thread fall on a base fabric and are set in place with a sheer overlay. The playful, decorative result makes the perfect border for a duvet cover, a placemat, pillow, or to add a dash of easy chic to a simple top.

light- to medium-weight woven fabric for the base

heavyweight thread or embroidery floss for "drawing" on the fabric

scraps of fabric in complementary colors

sheer silk or cotton fabric such as voile, georgette, or organza

lightweight iron-on adhesive
or
fusible adhesive

thread to match base fabric

lint-free pressing cloth or baking parchment

handsewing needle

ruler or tape measure

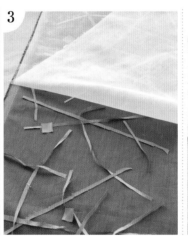
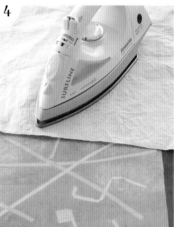

NOTE: If you plan to make the Top with a Border, skip to p. 64 for yardage requirements and cutting instructions before following the instructions below.

stitchless embroidery

1) Cut the sheer fabric with very sharp scissors to the width you want for your border (I made a 10" (25.5 cm) wide border). Cut fusible adhesive to the same size as the sheer fabric. Protect your iron and ironing surface by placing the sheer fabric and adhesive between 2 pieces of baking parchment or 2 pressing cloths and then follow the manufacturer's instructions to fuse the adhesive to the wrong side of the sheer fabric.

2) Cut strips, swatches, and snips of fabric in whatever shapes you desire and lay them down on the border in the desired pattern on the base fabric. Or try the ideas on p. 63 that use cut shapes of fabric and thread to experiment with other patterns.

3) Lay the sheer fabric, adhesive side down, onto the base fabric in the spot where you would like the design. Be sure that all assorted pieces (fabric and/or thread) of the design are covered by the sheer fabric.

4) Using a lint-free pressing cloth or baking parchment to protect your iron, follow the manufacturer's instructions to fuse the sheer fabric down to the base, capturing the design between the base and the sheer fabric. The sheer fabric will mute the color of the base fabric and the stitchless embroidery design, forming a well-defined border. Let the area cool and dry.

NOTE: The adhesives are generally washable so the adhesive and the design remain fixed through multiple (gentle) washings. However, the sheer fabric allows some adhesive to ooze through its surface so always use a pressing cloth when you subsequently iron the border to avoid damaging the iron or the fabric.

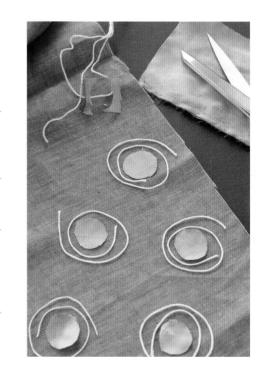

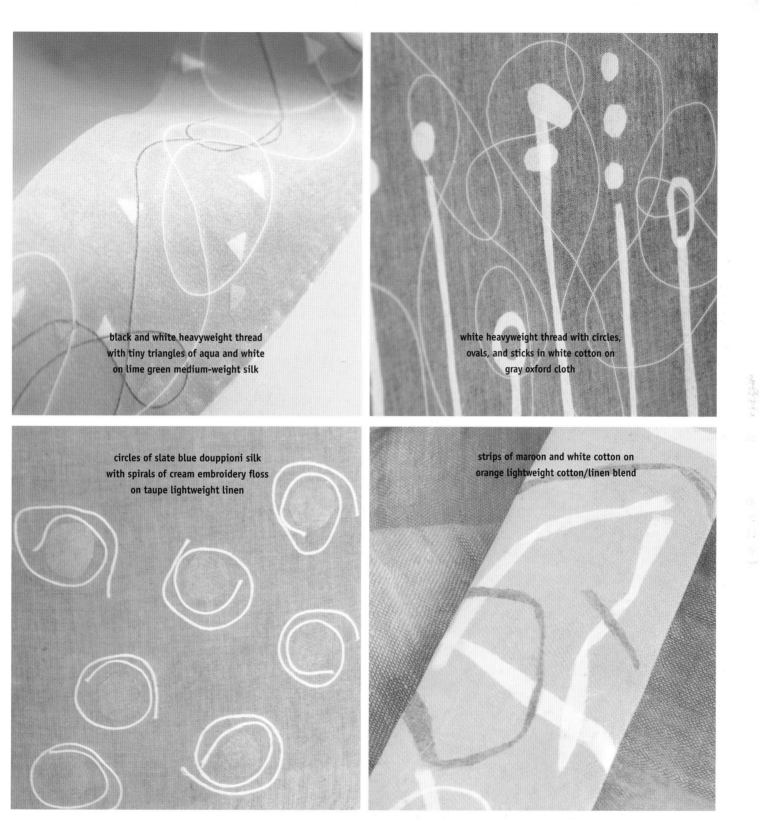

black and white heavyweight thread
with tiny triangles of aqua and white
on lime green medium-weight silk

white heavyweight thread with circles,
ovals, and sticks in white cotton on
gray oxford cloth

circles of slate blue douppioni silk
with spirals of cream embroidery floss
on taupe lightweight linen

strips of maroon and white cotton on
orange lightweight cotton/linen blend

materials

²/₃ yd (61 cm) of light- to medium-weight woven fabric for the base (at least 45" [117 cm] wide; I used light green)

heavyweight thread or embroidery floss for "drawing" on the fabric

scraps of fabric in complementary colors

⅛ yd (11.5 cm) sheer silk or cotton fabric, such as voile, georgette, or organza (at least 45" [117 cm] wide)

lightweight iron-on adhesive or fusible adhesive

sewing thread to match base fabric

toolbox

In addition to the tools listed on p. 62, you will need:

Pinking shears (optional)

finished size

S (M, L) is sized to fit a 31½–33½ (34–36, 37–38½)" (80–84 [86.5–91.5, 94–98] cm) bust circumference. Top shown is size S.

cut and stitch

NOTE: This top is meant to be loose and comfortable, but you may find that you'd like to customize the fit, especially as the lower ends of each size range (above) will have quite a bit of ease. To create a slightly more fitted top, once the side seams have been sewn, try on the top inside out. Determine how closely you would like the top to fit and pin (or have someone pin for you) down the side seam at that point, taking care that the pins run in a straight line, parallel to the original seam. Take in the side seams by sewing along the pinned line, then trim away the excess fabric from the seam allowance. Be sure that the finished measurement of the top is at least 2–3" (5–7.5 cm) larger than your bust circumference (the pinned side seams will each be at least 1–1½" [2.5–3.8 cm] away from your body at the bust) to maintain the easy-fit style of the top and ensure ease of slipping the top on and off over your head.

top with a border

1) Using the pattern template on p. 122 (S) or 123 (M, L), cut out 2 of the pattern pieces, one each for the Front and the Back (the front and back of the top are the same). Be sure to place the pattern piece on the fold when cutting each piece. The pattern template already includes the ½" (1.3 cm) seam allowance.

2) Create a sheer overlay border of the desired width (mine is 4" [10 cm] wide) along the bottom edge of the Front and Back pattern pieces following the instructions on p. 62. Be sure that the edges are cut very straight and that the border goes right to the bottom and to each side of the pattern piece (see diagram above).

3) With right sides (p. 120) together, pin the Front and Back pieces together along the sides and at the shoulder seams.

4) Sew the side seams, starting at the underarm and stopping at the top of the sheer overlay border created in Step 2. You will leave the side seam open here to make vents for ease of movement. Sew the shoulder seams together. Press all seams open, then finish with the zigzag stitch (p. 120) on your sewing machine or pink the edges.

5) Create a rolled hem at the neckline and armholes by folding the fabric under (toward the wrong side) about ¼" (6 mm), then roll that over another ¼" (6 mm) so that the raw edge is inside the fold. Pin to secure.

6) Handstitch the rolled neckline and armhole hems with a running stitch (p. 121), about ⅛" (3 mm) from the edge. Make sure the stitches that show on the outside of the top are tinier than the ones on the inside of the hem. Neatness counts; try to keep the stitches even and straight.

7) Fold under the ½" (1.3 cm) seam allowance at the side vents and pin. Handstitch as in Step 6, about ¼" (6 mm) from the edge.

8) Create a small rolled hem at the bottom of the border and handstitch as in Step 6. Now you have a finished top with clean finished edges!

NOTES: All seam allowances are ½" (1.3 cm) unless otherwise indicated.

If you are looking for a portable project that can be done without a sewing machine, this one is perfect. Only the side seams are sewn by machine and those short seams could easily be sewn by hand, making this the perfect project-on-the-go.

1

2

3

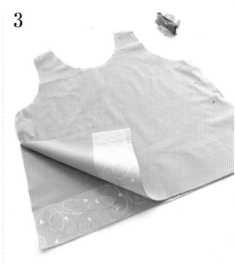

4

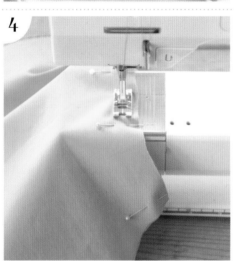

5

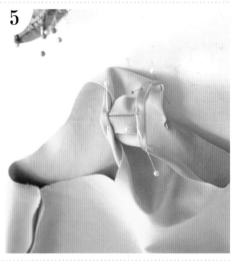

6

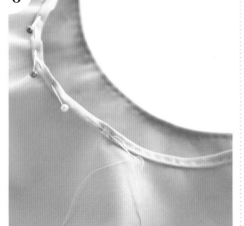

7

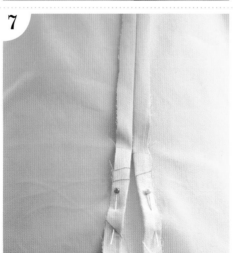

8

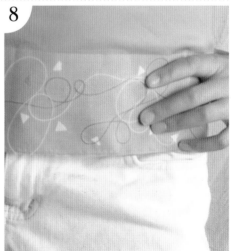

swatch MATRIX

This technique takes the most humble muslin and transforms it into something edgy and modern. A fluttering mass of triangles or squares is randomly crazy-stitched together into a gossamer matrix. Its true character shines when light comes through it, showing off the intriguing geometry of angular shapes and stitching. Make the lampshade (instructions on p. 70), or try a curtain panel or room-dividing screen. Even without electricity, this technique can be used to light up a room.

materials

water-soluble stitch stabilizer

unbleached muslin

white or cream sewing thread

stiff interfacing such as Timtex

toolbox

spray bottle

spray starch (optional)

handsewing needle

NOTE: If you plan to create the Flying Swatches Lamp, skip to p. 70 for yardage requirements and swatch matrix measurements before following the instructions below.

swatch matrix

1) Cut 2 pieces of dissolvable stitch stabilizer to the desired finished size of your swatch matrix fabric (one each for the top and bottom).

2) Cut long strips of cotton muslin in ¾, 1, and 1½" (2, 2.5, and 3.8 cm) widths. Cut the end of one of the strips on the diagonal to make a triangle shape. Continue to cut the strips, on the diagonal, creating triangles in three different sizes. You'll need quite a stack of each size to make a solid fabric (½ yd [46 cm] of muslin enough for a swatch matrix measuring 29 x 15" [73.5 x 38 cm] to make the lamp on p. 70).

3) Lay out the bottom piece of water-soluble stabilizer on a waterproof surface. (I used a plastic signboard so I could move it out of the way, but a worktable or countertop would be fine). Begin layering the cotton triangles randomly onto the stabilizer. It is important that the triangles not only touch each other but also overlap so that the fabric isn't too open and "thready" when you are done.

4) Once you are happy with the density of triangles, cover with the top layer of stabilizer.

5) There is really no way to pin all these triangles to the stabilizer without driving yourself crazy. Instead, spritz the stabilizer lightly with a spray bottle. Because the stabilizer is water soluble, spraying it with water will cause it to begin to melt and fuse together. Be sure to spray enough so that the top and bottom layers come together and "pin" the triangles in place. When dry you will have a single piece of stabilizer with the fabric sandwiched within.

6) Machine sew lines of stitching back and forth, crisscrossing the surface of the sandwiched matrix. You don't have to be too deliberate in your stitching, just prolific. It is best if the stitching doesn't leave any "holes" bigger than ½" (1.3 cm) across

7) Soak the fabric in cool water to melt away the stabilizer according to the manufacturer's directions.

8) Lay flat to dry. While fabric is still damp, iron flat. You can use spray starch for a stiffer finished product.

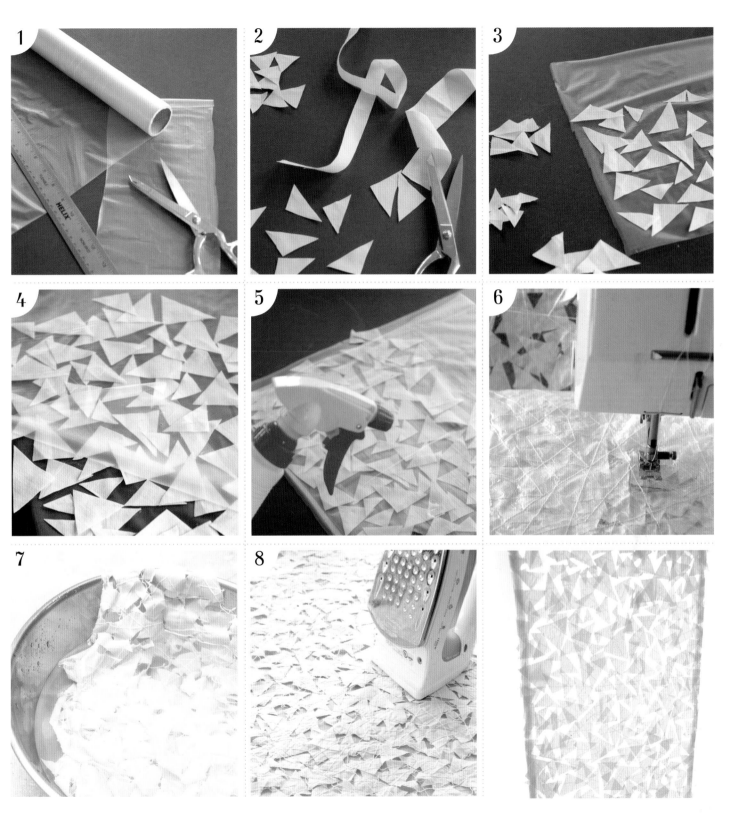

materials

1 yd (91.5 cm) of water-soluble
stitch stabilizer

½ yd (46 cm) of unbleached muslin

white or cream thread

56" (142 cm) of 1" (2.5 cm) wide single-
fold bias tape

¼ yd (23 cm) of stiff interfacing
such as Timtex

8" (20.5 cm) circular pendant light
and harp

toolbox

See tools listed on p. 68

finished size

15" (38 cm) long x 8" (20.5 cm)
in diameter

flying swatches lamp

1) Make a piece of swatch matrix fabric that is about 29 x 15"
(73.5 x 38 cm), according to the instructions on p. 68. Cut 2 strips
of stiff interfacing about ¼" (6 mm) wide x 29" (73.5 cm) long.
Position the interfacing along the long edges of the matrix fabric,
then roll the fabric over the interfacing to make a stiffer edge. Pin
and then machine sew with a straight or zigzag stitch (p. 120).

2) Enclose the stiffened edge in bias tape to cover and finish the
edge: fold the bias tape in half and press, then insert the stiffened
edge of the fabric into the fold. Pin in place, then stitch down the
length through all layers, about ⅜" (1 cm) from the outside edge
(see diagram A, at left).

3) Now attach one of the bound edges of the fabric to the lamp
harp; place the edge of the fabric a little above the harp so that it
is covered.

4) Handstitch the bound edge to the harp by whipstitching (p. 121)
through the binding and around the harp every few inches, working
your way all the way around the perimeter of the harp.
The ends of the binding will overlap about ½" (1.3 cm).

To finish) Overlap remaining swatch matrix fabric to create a back
seam down the lamp shade. Handsew down the length of the over-
lapped back seam to close the cylinder, using a whipstitch at intervals,
wherever you have swatches overlapping. Try to hide the stitches in
the existing stitching on the fabric. If there is too much overlap, cut
away any excess fabric. You will now have a round lampshade attached to the 8" (20.5 cm) harp (see diagram B, at left).

cut and stitch

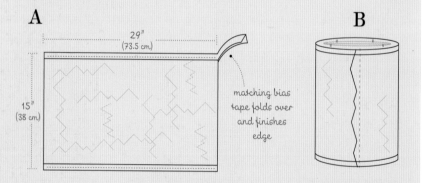

A

29"
(73.5 cm)

15"
(38 cm)

matching bias
tape folds over
and finishes
edge

B

1

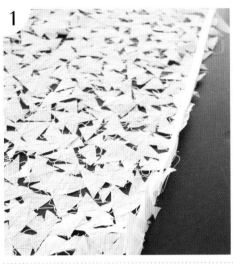

2

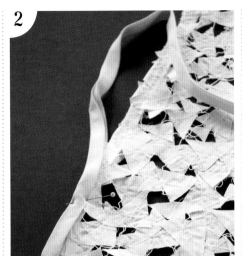

3

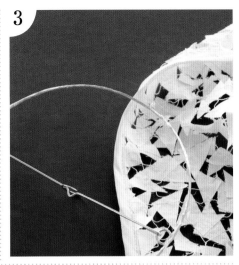

4

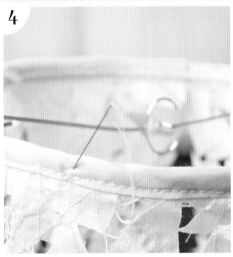

SAFE AND SMART:

To ensure that this lampshade is as safe and energy efficient as it is beautiful, please use only cool-burning compact fluorescent bulbs.

swirling FREELACE

O kay, so it might be a stretch to call this tangle of yarn, string, and thread "lace," but the delicate filigreed structure bears lots of similarities. The earthy textures and natural colors make this matrix look organic, like a bird's nest. On the surface, it has a casual dishevelment, but look closer and you'll see a careful organizing principle that underlies its swirling beauty. This placemat is an easy project that lets you borrow from your knitting stash and sew some yarn.

materials

water-soluble stitch stabilizer

scraps of natural fiber yarn and jute and cotton string

neutral colored sewing thread

toolbox

measuring tape or ruler

tub of water

finished placemat is about 14 x 20" (35.5 x 51 cm)
sew a vertical and horizontal grid
with stitching at ½" (1.3 cm) intervals

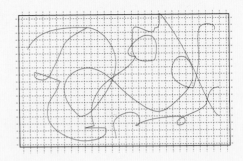

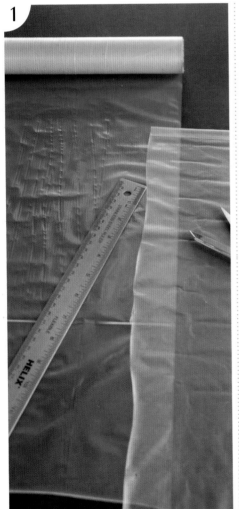

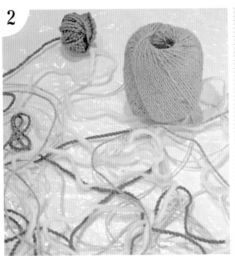

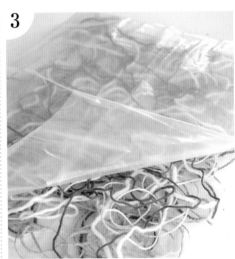

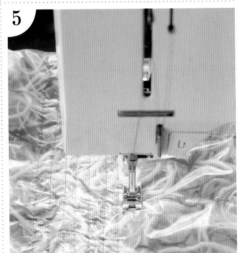

swirling freelace

1) Measure and cut 2 pieces of stabilizer to the desired size for your project. Lay the first piece out flat.

2) Lay swirling loops of various yarns and string over the entire surface of the stabilizer, being sure to cover the surface fairly evenly.

3) Add the top piece of stabilizer over the first, sandwiching the yarns and string in between.

4) Pin the whole sandwiched matrix together at either edge and with at least 3 rows of pins down the center (increase the number of pinned rows if you have a very large piece; just be sure the pieces of stabilizer are securely held together).

5) Topstitch (p.120) across the matrix at ½" (1.3 cm) intervals, first going one way, then turning the piece 90 degrees and sewing at ½" (1.3 cm) intervals in the other direction, across the first set of stitch lines.

To finish) Submerge the piece in cool water to dissolve the stabilizer according to the manufacturer's instructions. Let dry flat.

placemat

To create the placemat shown here, measure and cut 2 pieces of stabilizer, each about 14 x 20" (35.5 x 51 cm). Follow the instructions at left to create a lovely organic-looking placemat.

PART THREE

CUT & FRAY

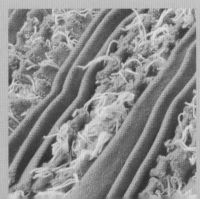

silk CHENILLE

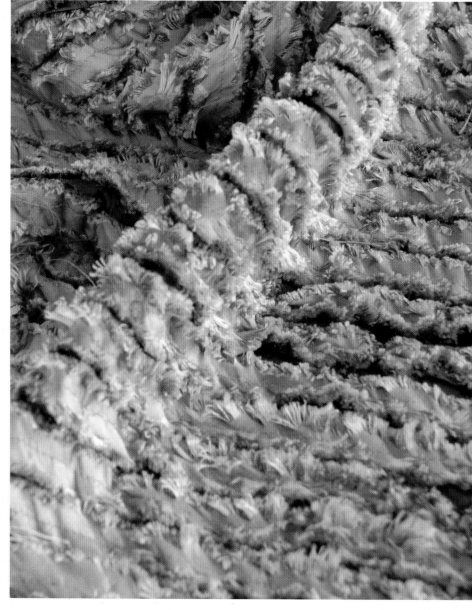

This must be why the silkworm weaves the cocoon—to feel enveloped in plush, weightless silken softness. This fabric employs an ancient medieval technique of layering, then slashing, then fraying the material to create a luxuriant pile. The closest thing to it is chenille (literally "caterpillar" in French), a soft, tufted fabric. This version, made with four layers of douppioni silk, is nothing like the bedspread and bathrobe chenille of our childhood. This is molten silk flowing across your skin, a shimmering cloud you can actually wear.

materials

100% silk douppioni in 4 colors

sewing thread

Fray Check (optional)

toolbox

yardstick

nonpermanent fabric marking pencil

washing machine and dryer

stiff natural-bristle brush

NOTE: If you plan to make the Faux Chenille Wrap, skip to p. 83 for yardage requirements and cutting dimensions before following the instructions below.

faux chenille

1) Cut the 4 colors of silk to the desired size for your project and stack them on top of each other, lining up all edges, with the color you would like to be the bottom layer placed at the top of the stack. Pin loosely to hold the pieces together.

2) Starting at one corner, measure down one side about 10" (25.5 cm) and make a mark with the pencil. Starting at the same corner, measure down the other side about 10" (25.5 cm) and mark. Place your yardstick on the marks and draw a diagonal line to connect the two. This line is running on the diagonal or "bias" of the fabric. Use your ruler to mark lines, parallel to this first one, at ⅝–¾" (1.5–2 cm) intervals, down the length of the fabric. Use pins along the length of the lines to hold the layers of fabric securely together.

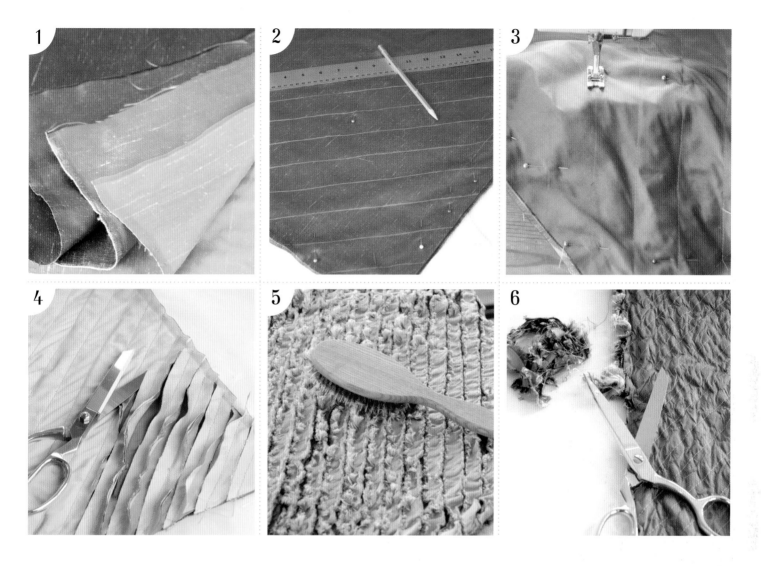

3) Machine stitch straight along the penciled lines keeping the fabric smooth as you go.

I used a yardstick that happened to measure 1½" (3.8 cm) wide. I used the width of the yardstick to mark every other line. After stitching the first set of lines, I could go back and eyeball a line of stitching halfway between the other two lines. This saved time and tedium in the marking process.

4) After stitching all the lines, flip the fabric over. Cut the channels between the stitching, halfway between each stitch line, cutting only through the top 3 layers. This is not a difficult process, but needs to be done with care so you don't cut through more layers than intended.

5) Machine wash and dry your piece with a load of jeans or towels that will create friction and help your fabric to fray and "bloom." You could do this several times, but you risk shrinking the silk if it is washed too frequently. Try using a clean stiff-bristled brush to bring up the fray. Brush briskly along the channels in both directions to create the amount of fraying you desire.

6)) Using sharp scissors, trim along the edges of the piece to make them straight and eliminate any excess threads. Use Fray Check on the base fabric edges, if desired.

materials

¾ yd (68.5 cm) each of 100% silk douppioni in 4 colors (at least 54" [137 cm] wide; I used purple, gray-blue, orange, and light green)

sewing thread

Fray Check (optional)

toolbox

See tools listed on p. 80

finished size

24" (61 cm) long x 54" (137 cm) wide

cut and stitch

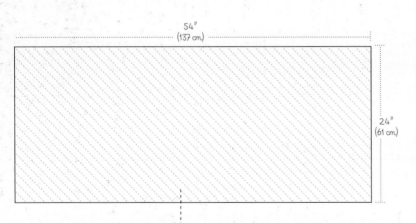

54"
(137 cm)

24"
(61 cm)

diagonal stitch lines every ⅝-¾" (1.5-2 cm)
*(stitching closer together makes a denser,
more luxuriant chenille, but it takes
longer to make . . . you decide)*

silk wrap

faux chenille wrap

Cut the 4 colors of silk to 24" (61 cm) long x 54" (137 cm) wide, then follow the instructions on pp. 82–83 to create the wrap. Adjust the cutting dimensions and yardage requirements if you would like a longer or shorter wrap.

NOTE: This wrap is 54" (137 cm) wide because that is a typical width for douppioni silk fabric. If you are happy with a wrap that is 54" (137 cm), then you can make this project using a very efficient ¾ yd (68.5 cm) of each color of silk.

frayed CIRCLES

Sometimes the simplest touch can make something come to life. These little tufts of earth-toned cotton and linen are full of natural character. Earthy, organic, they are like airborne seedpods, or pussy willows, or some fluttering winged creature attracted to the light and airy windowsill. Stitched to a sheer curtain, they are right at home rustling and floating on the slightest breeze.

materials

sheer cotton fabric such as voile for base

3–5 varieties of 100% cotton, linen, or silk for tufts (about ⅛ yd [11.5 cm] each of 5 fabrics should be sufficient for the Sheer Curtain on p. 88)

embroidery floss or sewing thread

assorted small buttons (optional)

toolbox

measuring tape

handsewing or embroidery needle

small bowl of water

1

2

3

4

5

frayed circles

1) Cut rough circles out of the linen and/or silk fabrics in 2 basic sizes. The larger circles should be about 1½" (3.8 cm) in diameter; the smaller circles should be about ¾" (2 cm) in diameter.

2) Dunk the fabric circles in water to wet thoroughly.

3) Rub and wad each fabric circle vigorously between the palms of your hands. Reverse direction frequently as you rub to make sure the fabric is getting sufficiently rough treatment. Unwad the ball of fabric and check the edges for fraying. Continue rolling and wadding the fabric circles in your hands until they have developed a pleasant fringe around the edges.

4) When you undo the wads of fabric, don't smooth them out too much because wrinkles and crinkles are part of their charm. If you want more fraying, work your way around the edge pulling out threads as you go. Let the fabric circles dry completely.

5) You can use either an embroidery needle with embroidery floss or a handsewing needle and thread to gather and sew your tufts. Baste (p. 120) in a circle near the center of a fabric circle. Pull the thread to gather the fabric circle into a tight tuft and knot the thread to secure; do not trim thread. Repeat until all circles are gathered into tufts.

To finish) Stack a smaller circle tuft on top of a larger one and stitch them together through the middle with the thread from basting (Step 5). You can make a center for the tuft by sewing several stitches right on top of each other, or, alternatively, you can sew a button onto the center. Attach the tuft to the base fabric using a stitch or two on the back of the tuft. Tie off and trim thread.

sheer curtains

materials

sheer cotton fabric such as voile for curtain
(see instructions at right for measuring instructions to calculate yardage needed)

⅛ yd (11.5 cm) each of 3–5 varieties of 100% cotton, linen, or silk for tufts

embroidery floss or sewing thread

toolbox

see tools listed on p. 86

finished size

Curtain shown here is 48" (122 cm) long x 36" (91.5 cm) wide. Measure the window you wish to cover and follow the instructions at right to obtain the correct measurements for your own curtain.

cut and stitch

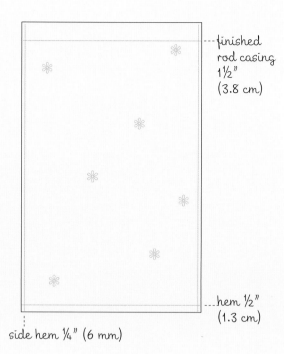

finished rod casing 1½" (3.8 cm)

hem ½" (1.3 cm)

side hem ¼" (6 mm)

sheer curtains

To start) Measure the window opening for your curtain. Mark curtain fabric at 1½ to 2 times as wide as your window measurement to create a full, billowy curtain. Add an extra 1" (2.5 cm) to the width for side hems and an extra 2¼" (5.5 cm) to the length to account for the casing and the hem, then cut out the curtain panels. Follow the instructions on p. 86 to create and attach the frayed circles to the curtain. Attach as many as you would like in a random pattern to create the desired effect (see the diagram at left).

1) To finish the curtain's side seams, fold one edge of the fabric over ¼" (6 mm) toward the wrong side (p. 120), then fold it over ¼" (6 mm) onto itself again to make a ¼" (6 mm) wide rolled hem, with no raw edges exposed. Pin to hold in place. Topstitch (p. 120) along the side of the curtain, about ⅛" (3 mm) from the edge. Repeat on the opposite side of curtain.

2) To create the curtain-rod casing at the top of the curtain, mark a line 1¾" (4.5 cm) down from the top edge. Fold the top edge of the fabric down ¼" (6 mm) toward the wrong side, then turn that folded edge down to your marked line (this will eliminate the raw edge). Pin and topstitch ¼" (6 mm) from the inside edge. Adjust these measurements depending on the size of your curtain rod if necessary. Make a rolled hem at the bottom of the curtain, as in Step 1.

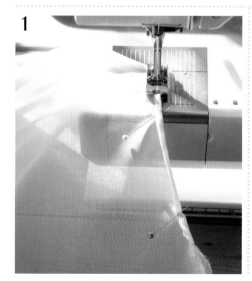

1

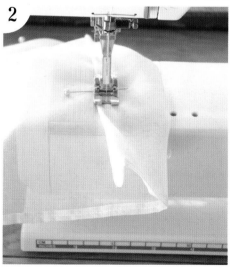

2

tumbled FRAYS

Cut a rug? You bet. This project uses one of the best aspects of denim: the way it frays after it is cut and washed. The rug is thick and plush and cushy and tough— all at the same time. This is a surface that begs for bare feet. Its surprising texture makes you want to linger. And the best news is that it wants to be thrown in the washing machine. Like a good pair of jeans, this instant classic takes in stride the wear and tear of modern life. It just gets better and better with each new fray.

cut and stitch

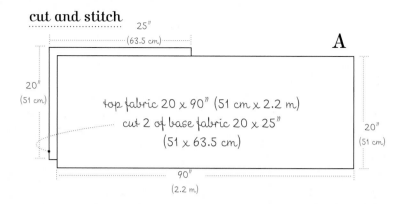

A

25" (63.5 cm)

20" (51 cm)

top fabric 20 x 90" (51 cm x 2.2 m)
cut 2 of base fabric 20 x 25"
(51 x 63.5 cm)

20" (51 cm)

20" (51 cm)

90" (2.2 m)

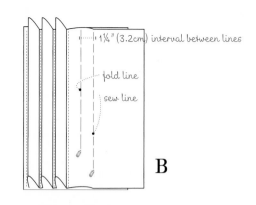

B

1¼" (3.2cm) interval between lines

fold line

sew line

materials

2½ yd (2.3 m) cotton denim fabric

matching sewing thread

toolbox

ruler

fabric marking pencil

washing machine and dryer

tennis shoe (optional)

size 75/11 sewing machine needle for sewing on denim (optional)

finished size

20 x 25" (51 x 63.5 cm).

NOTE:
All seam allowances are ½" (1.3 cm) unless otherwise indicated.

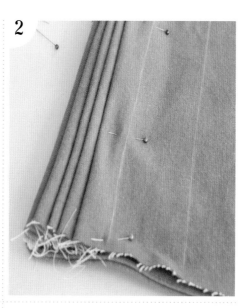

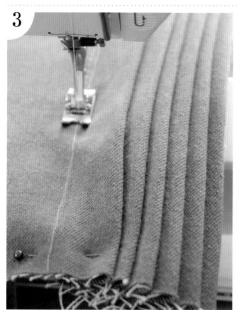

tumbled frays rug

To start) Cut a 20 x 90" (51 cm x 2.2 m) rectangle of denim for the top fabric (alternatively, you can cut 2 rectangles, each measuring 20 x 45½" [51 x 115.5 cm] and seam them together, because this seam can easily be hidden in the final product); set aside. Make a base for the tumbled fray pile by cutting 2 pieces of denim, each measuring 21 x 26" (53.5 x 66 cm). With right sides (p. 120) together, sew the 2 pieces together on all sides, leaving a 6" (15 cm) gap along one edge. Turn the piece right side out, through the gap. Tuck in the raw edges and machine stitch closed.

Lay the top fabric right side up on the base and topstitch (p. 120) the pieces together along the short edge (see diagram A at left). Because this fabric is all about fraying, there is no need to finish any of the edges on the top fabric.

1) Mark a line parallel to the stitch line just made, 1¼" (3.2 cm) from the stitch line. Mark another parallel line 1¼" (3.2 cm) from the first. The first line is a folding guide; the second is a stitch guide. Fold the fabric along the first line to form a pleat that is about ½" (1.3 cm) at the base and pin in place along the second line (see diagram B at left). Topstitch along the stitch line, through all 3 layers of fabric, to secure the pleat.

2) Mark the next set of pleats, fold, and sew as in Step 1. Continue to mark, fold, pin, and sew the pleats in place in this manner, all the way across the top fabric. Make sure that each pleat is about ½" (1.3 cm) wide (this will leave about ⅜" [1 cm] between each pleat). It is best to fold and stitch the pleats as you go (rather than marking the whole length first) because it is easy to get off by a centimeter here and there. Those centimeters can add up quickly and it is easier to adjust, if necessary, as you go.

3) Continue making pleats until the entire base fabric is covered. When you reach the end, topstitch the edge of the top fabric to the edge of the base, as before.

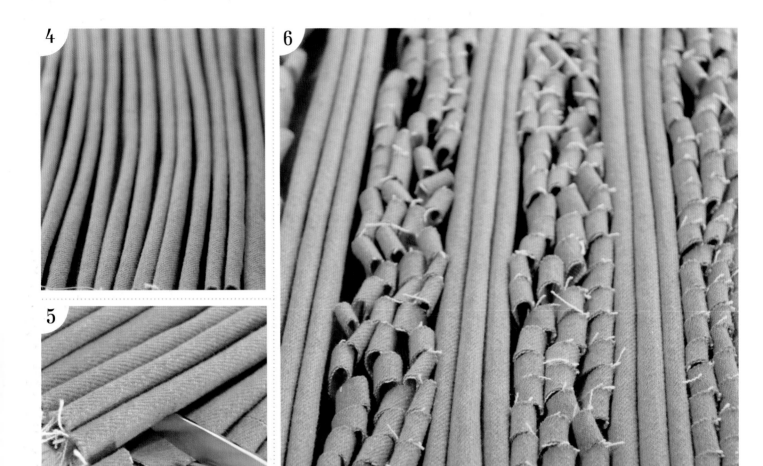

Before continuing, read Steps 4 and 5.

4) With very sharp scissors, begun cutting the sewn pleats at ½–¾" (1.3–2 cm) intervals, along the length of the pleats, to make loops. Be sure to cut only about 1" (2.5 cm) down into each pleat, taking care not to cut through the stitches or nip the base fabric.

5) To create the interesting texture on this rug, cut every 3 or 4 rows of pleats and then leave the next 2, 3, or 4 rows uncut. This creates a pattern that makes the finished rug look more graphic and purposeful in appearance.

To finish) To fray the finished rug, put it through a hot-water cycle in the washing machine, followed by a long tumble in the dryer with a tennis shoe or something similar (to create resistance), roughing up the surface. Because the rug is made from all the same material, even a little shrinkage shouldn't be a problem: everything will shrink at the same rate. This rug will improve with frequent laundering.

tumbled
frays
rug

PART FOUR

SURFACE EMBELLISHMENT

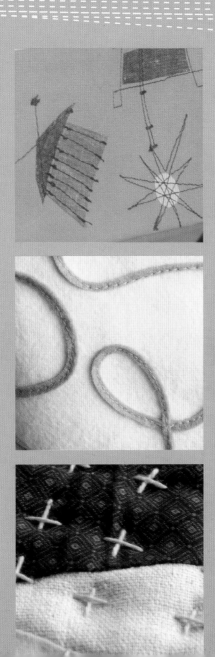

machine APPLIQUÉ

Oh boy! This is more fun than you're supposed to have as a grown up. Inspired by a fabric from the 1950s in the collection of the Victoria and Albert Museum in London, this retro folly seems complex. But if you break it down slowly, adding a simple scrap of fabric here and some converging lines of stitching there, before you know it, you have created a crazy/wonderful fabric illustration. Apply it to a handy messenger bag and you're good to go!

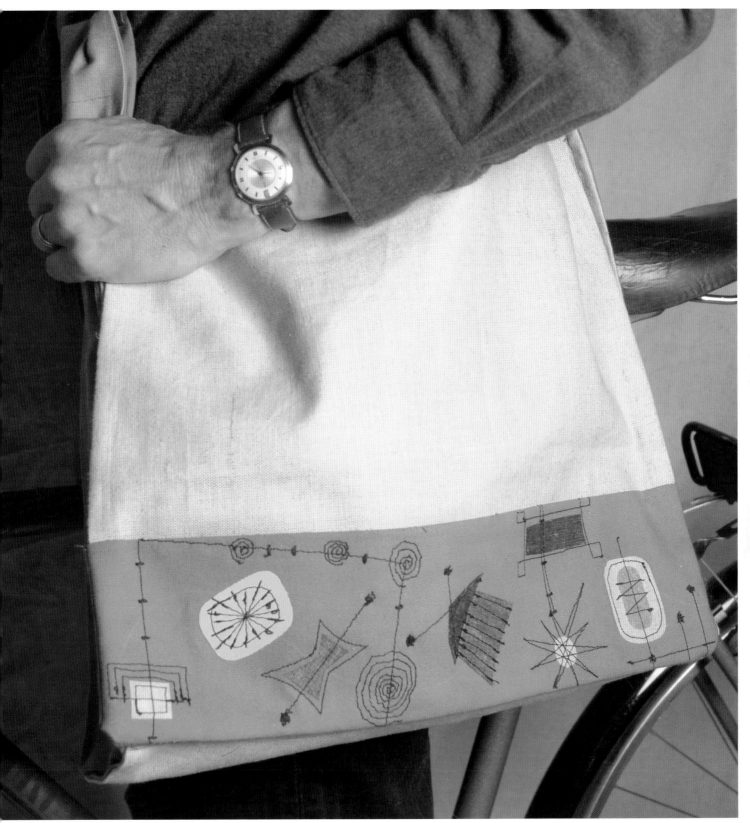

materials

about ¼ yd (23 cm) each
of various colors
of light- to medium-
weight cotton or linen
(if you plan to make a
large piece, adjust yardage
as necessary)

iron-on adhesive
(enough to cover all of
the above fabrics)

black heavyweight
sewing thread

cotton duck for base

sewing thread in color to
match base

size 90/14 sewing machine
needle for topstitched
embellishment

toolbox

nonpermanent fabric
marking pen or pencil

ruler

NOTE: If you plan to create the
Messenger Bag, skip to pages
102–103 for yardage requirements and cutting dimensions
before following the
instructions at right.

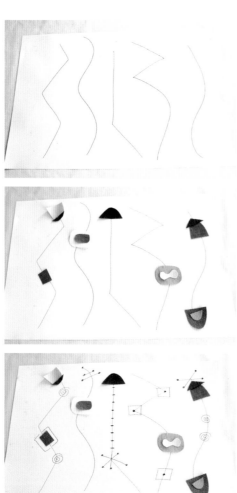

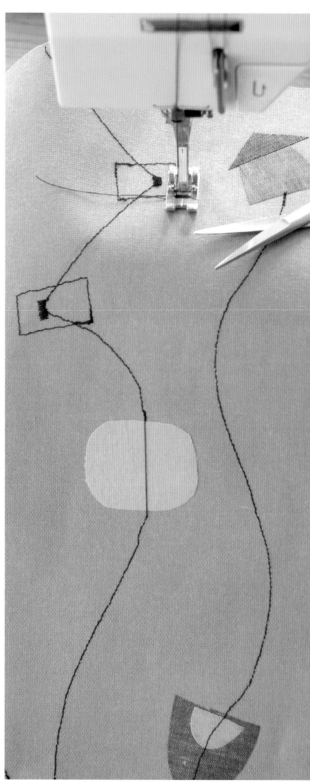

machine appliqué

To start) It's simple to come up with a pleasing
design when you start out with simple shapes and
fill in a few repeating whimsical motifs. Begin with a
sheet of paper, cut to the desired size of your finished
piece and play with the layout of your appliqué
design before transferring it to the fabric. You can use
colored paper to cut out shapes or follow the instructions on p. 101 to prepare the fabric and then cut out
your fabric shapes. Use a pen or pencil to draw in the
stitch lines. The illustration above starts with 5 simple
lines, then gets livelier with the addition of a few basic
shapes, then really jumps off the page with the addition of dots, spirals, and intersecting lines.

1

2

3

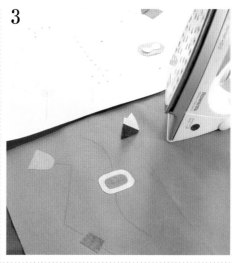

4

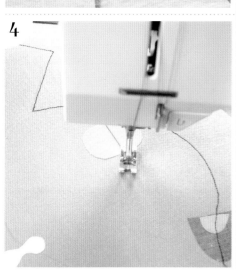

5a

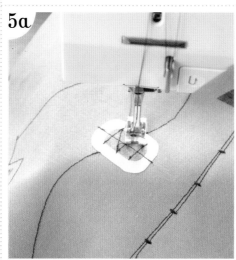

5b

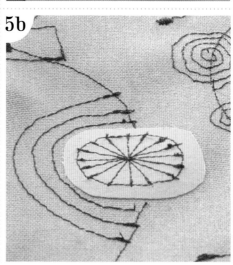

1) Following the manufacturer's instructions, iron the adhesive to the wrong sides of your various colors of cotton or linen.

2) Cut the desired simple shapes out of the resulting fabric. Some good ones are domed rectangles, mushroom shapes, rounded rectangles, ovals, and triangles.

3) Cut the base fabric to the desired size of your finished piece. Draw the main lines on your base fabric (having practiced earlier on the sheet of paper) with the fabric marking pen or pencil. Following the manufacturer's instructions, iron the adhesive-backed shapes into place on your fabric, placing them as desired.

4) Using the heavyweight thread, topstitch (p. 120) along the drawn lines to begin.

5) Embellishing and drawing on the fabric requires a small number of stitching techniques that can be used over and over again. Use bar tacks (zigzag stitch [p. 120] where the presser foot doesn't move forward) to make "dots" on the fabric. Use the back-tack (stitching backwards) on your machine to darken lines and corners. Fill in rectangles with stitching that goes back and forth (5a) and use lots of lines that cross or converge (5b). Outline the various fabric pieces with boxes, circles, and spirals. A simple technique you will use a lot is to leave your needle down at the end of a segment, pivot the

fabric around that point, and stitch off in another direction. To make spirals, spin your fabric slowly as you sew to guide the stitching into a spiral shape. Just play and try things. It doesn't take much to make an energetic and fun illustration. Use the samples shown here for inspiration.

Keep scissors handy to clip threads often.

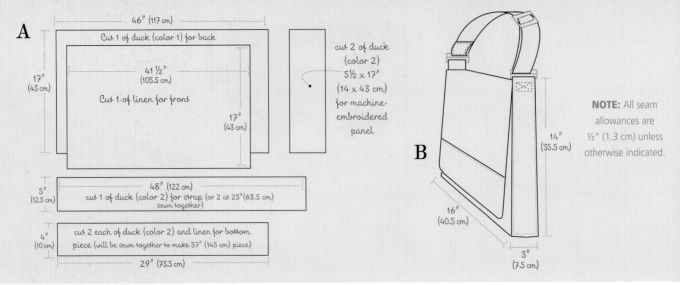

A

46" (117 cm)

Cut 1 of duck (color 1) for back

41½" (105.5 cm)

Cut 1 of linen for front

17" (43 cm)

17" (43 cm)

17" (43 cm)

cut 2 of duck (color 2) 5½ x 17" (14 x 43 cm) for machine-embroidered panel

48" (122 cm)
cut 1 of duck (color 2) for strap (or 2 at 25" (63.5 cm) sewn together)

5" (12.5 cm)

4" (10 cm)

cut 2 each of duck (color 2) and linen for bottom piece (will be sewn together to make 57" (145 cm) piece)

29" (73.5 cm)

B

14" (35.5 cm)

16" (40.5 cm)

3" (7.5 cm)

NOTE: All seam allowances are ½" (1.3 cm) unless otherwise indicated.

materials

about ¼ yd (23 cm) each of various colors of light- to medium-weight cotton or linen

iron-on adhesive (enough to cover all of the above fabrics)

black heavyweight sewing thread

1½ yd (1.4 m) of cotton duck (color 1—I used green)

½ yd (46 cm) of heavyweight linen (I used natural)

1 yd (91.5 cm) of cotton duck (color 2—I used reddish brown)

matching sewing thread

three 3" (7.5 cm) wooden buckles

toolbox

in addition to the tools listed on p. 101, you will need:

fabric marking pen or pencil

handsewing needle

finished size:

14" (35.5 cm) tall x 16" (40.5 cm) wide x 3" (7.5 cm) deep. Strap is adjustable from 25–46" (63.5–117 cm).

retro messenger bag

To start) See diagram A at left for assistance. Cut the following pieces:

- One 17 x 46" (43 x 117 cm) rectangle of cotton duck (color 1) for lining.

- One 17 x 41½" (43 x 105.5 cm) rectangle of linen for body of bag.

- One 5 x 48" (12.5 x 122 cm) rectangle of duck (color 2) for shoulder strap (if your fabric is not wide enough to cut 1 piece, cut 2 pieces that are 24½" [62 cm] long instead, then sew them together at one short end to create the 48" [122 cm] long piece).

- Four 4 x 29" (10 x 73.5 cm) rectangles, 2 each of duck (color 2) and linen, for gusset.

- Two 17 x 5½" (43 x 14 cm) rectangles of duck (color 2) for border. Use one to create the machine appliqué border, leave the other plain.

Follow the instructions on p. 101 to create the machine appliqué border, using the 17 x 5½" (43 x 14 cm) rectangle.

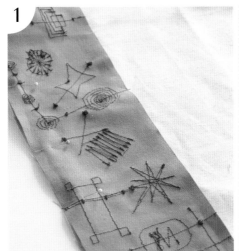

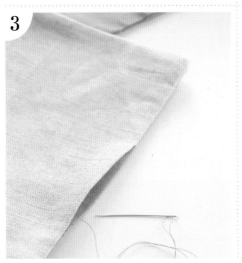

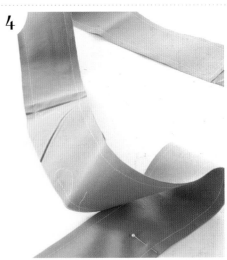

1) With right sides (p. 120) together, pin and sew the completed machine-appliqué border to one short end of the linen shell piece. Press seam flat. Repeat entire step to attach the unembellished border to the duck lining piece.

2) With right sides together, pin and sew the bordered linen piece to the bordered duck lining (match up the borders) on all 4 sides, leaving a 5" (12.5 cm) gap on the top edge to turn. Trim corners as shown, and zigzag (p. 120) edge if fabric is prone to ravel.

3) Turn the piece right side out. Tuck in the raw edges on the gap and handsew closed with a slip stitch (p. 121). Press the piece flat.

4) Place the 2 duck 4 x 29" (10 x 73.5 cm) rectangles with right sides together and sew them together along one short edge to make one long piece measuring 4 x 57" (10 x 145 cm). Repeat with the linen rectangles. Make the gusset (p. 120) piece by placing the two 4 x 57" (10 x 145 cm) rectangles right sides together and sewing around all 4 sides, leaving a gap open in the middle of the long seam to turn. Trim the seams to about ¼" (6 mm) and turn the gusset right side out. Tuck in the raw edges and handsew closed as in Step 3.

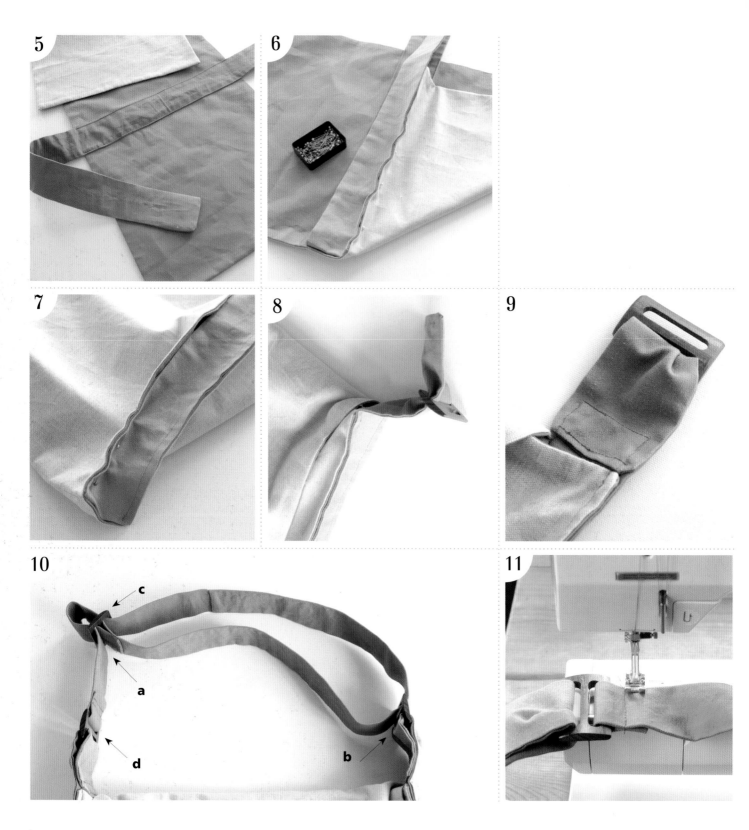

5) Lay the main body piece of the bag face down (with lining facing you); measure 14" (35.5 cm) down from the nonbordered edge and mark. Place the gusset (p. 120) piece, linen side down on the body piece, with the top of the gusset at the mark. Center the gusset side to side on the fabric and pin in place. Sew the gusset into place on the main body piece, stitching along the edges of the gusset from one side of the main body piece to the other. Stitch as close to the edges of the gusset as possible (about ¹⁄₁₆" [2 mm]).

6) Bend both the gusset and the main body piece up from the point where they meet and pin them together, as shown. This will form one corner of the front of the bag. Pin the gusset to the bag all the way up the front of the bag. The seam will be to the outside here and will show all 4 layers of fabric. Topstitch (p. 120) this seam. The gusset will extend about 7" (18 cm) beyond the top of the bag body.

7) Now, turn up the other side of the main bag body along the opposite edge of the gusset as shown. Pin and sew as in Step 6. Repeat on the other side of the bag to complete the remaining two side seams. The longer side of the main body of the bag will form the flap.

8) Add 1 wooden buckle to each of the gusset pieces extending over the top of the bag body.

9) Fold each gusset over toward the inside of the bag, trapping one side of the buckle in the fold. Align the edge of each gusset with the top of the bag body and pin in place. Topstitch the doubled layer of the gusset together with a rectangle of stitching that lines up with the previous stitching, as shown here.

10) Fold the shoulder strap piece in half lengthwise, pin and sew the long edge and one short edge, leaving one end open for the turn. Turn the strap right side out, then tuck in the raw edges and handsew closed with a slip stitch (p. 121).

See diagram B on p. 102 for further assistance with the following instructions. Thread the strap over the middle bar of the third wooden buckle so that the middle bar is trapped between the two sides of the strap (a). Sew in place with two lines of stitching, through both layers of the strap parallel to the short edge. Thread the strap through the top slot of the right-hand buckle from the inside to the outside (b), then loop back through the third buckle over the side of the strap previously attached (c), then down through the top slot of the left-hand buckle from the outside to the inside (d). Finish by folding the strap back up onto itself to the inside, around the top slot of the left-hand buckle.

11) Sew the strap in place with two lines of stitching as in Step 8.

applied FELT

This is not your grade-school teacher's felt. In the modern stitcher's toolkit, 100% wool felt is one of the most versatile and easy-to-work-with materials. Scrumptiously soft and with a very civilized amount of fuzziness, it can be cut, pieced, and appliquéd in thousands of ways without a single worry about finishing raw edges. Felt has been used in industrial applications for centuries, and this legacy has produced a distinctly utilitarian, no-nonsense edge that is a perfect foil for these whimsical and lighthearted appliqués.

1

2

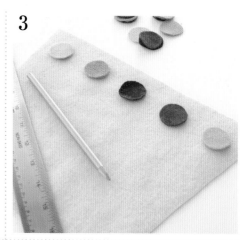

3

4

5

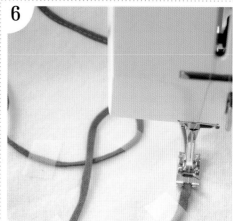

6

applied felt

1) Cut out the background felt to the size and shape of your project.

2) Trace a circle that is ¾–1 " (2 –2.5 cm) in diameter onto a piece of cardboard or chipboard (this is the stuff cereal boxes are made of). Cut out the circle with craft scissors. Use this template to cut out colored felt circles for the project. You'll want a couple dozen to start.

3) Lay the circles onto the background fabric in a straight line at comfortable intervals so they fill in across the surface. I have found that a ¾" (2 cm) gap between 1" (2.5 cm) circles looks good. Be sure to leave room for the seam allowance of your project. It is nice if all the circles still show as full circles after seams are sewn.

4) Continue to place the circles onto the background felt until you have the desired amount (for the Dots Bag on p. 110, be sure that the circles are placed in equally spaced lines down the length of the background felt). Pin the circles in place with all the pins going in the same direction so they will be easier to sew over.

5) With black or another contrasting color of sewing thread, topstitch (p. 120) through the center of the circles, first horizontally, then vertically, making a grid across the entire surface of the fabric.

6) To make swirls, cut long, thin strips of felt (about ⅛–³⁄₁₆" [3–5 mm] wide for the Swirl Bag on p. 110) of felt using scissors or a rotary cutter. Place these strips

onto the background fabric as desired, with lots of pleasing loops and swirls. The strips should always start and finish at an edge. Transparent tape works well to hold the swirls in place for sewing (pins create too much pucker). It is best to remove the tape right before sewing over it (put the tape on with light pressure so it is easy to pull off without pulling up the swirls). Use either a matching or contrasting color of sewing thread to topstitch along the length of the fabric strips to secure. Go slowly so you can easily follow the swirls you created and stay in the center of the strip.

materials

100% wool felt for background

a small amount of 100% wool felt in several colors (for dots) or one color (for swirls)

black (or matching) sewing thread

small piece of cardboard or chipboard

toolbox

craft scissors

ruler

transparent tape (optional)

NOTES: The instructions on p. 111 for using circles and swirls offer a few examples to get you started, but you can use many different shapes of felt for this technique.

If you plan to create either the Dot Bag or the Swirl Bag, skip to p. 110 for cutting dimensions before following the instructions below to apply the felt embellishment.

cut and stitch

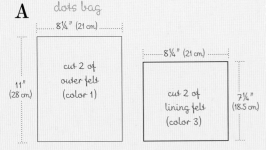

A dots bag

8¼" (21 cm)

11" (28 cm)

cut 2 of outer felt (color 1)

8¼" (21 cm)

cut 2 of lining felt (color 3)

7¼" (18.5 cm)

B swirl bag

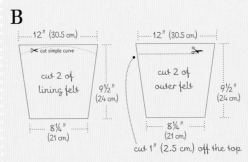

12" (30.5 cm)

✂ cut simple curve

cut 2 of lining felt

9½" (24 cm)

8¼" (21 cm)

12" (30.5 cm)

✂

cut 2 of outer felt

9½" (24 cm)

8¼" (21 cm)

cut 1" (2.5 cm) off the top

C both bags

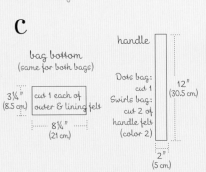

bag bottom
(same for both bags)

3¼" (8.5 cm)

cut 1 each of outer & lining felt

8¼" (21 cm)

handle

Dots bag: cut 1
Swirls bag: cut 2 of handle felt (color 2)

12" (30.5 cm)

2" (5 cm)

dots bag

materials

½ yd (46 cm) of 100% wool felt for main bag (color 1—I used natural)

⅓ yd (30.5 cm) of 100% wool felt in a contrasting color for handles (color 2—I used yellow)

½ yd (46 cm) of 100% wool felt in contrasting color for lining (color 3—I used red)

about ⅛ yd (12 cm) each of 100% wool felt in several colors (for Dots Bag), or one color (for Swirls Bag)

black (or matching) sewing thread

small piece of cardboard or chipboard (for Dots Bag)

toolbox

In addition to the tools listed on p. 109, you will need:

handsewing needle

finished size

DOTS BAG: 9" (23 cm) tall x 7¾" (19.5 cm) wide x 2¾" (7 cm) deep. With handle, bag is about 12" (30.5 cm) tall.

SWIRLS BAG: 9" (23 cm) tall x 12" (30.5 cm) wide at top x 2¾" (7 cm) deep. With handles, bag is about 11" (28 cm) tall.

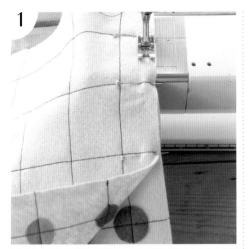

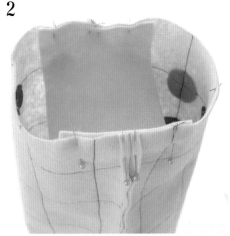

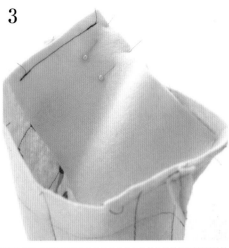

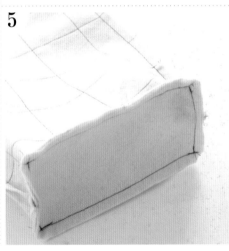

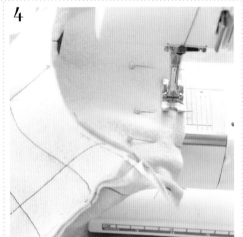

NOTE: All seam allowances are ½" (1.3 cm) unless otherwise indicated.

dots bag

To start) See diagrams A and C at left for assistance. Cut two 11 x 8¼" (28 x 21 cm) rectangles of felt (color 1) for the main bag and two 7¼ x 8¼" (18.5 x 21 cm) rectangles of contrasting color felt for the lining (color 3); set aside. Cut two 3¼ x 8¼" (8.5 x 21 cm) rectangles for the bag bottom, one from the main bag fabric (color 1) and one from the contrasting color lining fabric (color 3); set aside. Cut one 12 x 2" (30.5 x 5 cm) rectangle of contrasting color felt for the handle (color 2); set aside.

Embellish the main bag fabric pieces according to the instructions on p. 108.

1) With right sides (p. 120) together, sew the front and back of the bag together along the side seams.

2) Find the center of one short side of the bag bottom piece. Match this point to one of the side seams and pin in place as shown. Repeat at the opposite side of the bag bottom, matching up to the remaining side seam of the bag.

3) Stitch the bottom and the sides together, leaving about ¼" (6 mm) at each edge of the bag bottom free of stitching, as shown. Reinforce the seams with back-tacking (stitching backward) at each end. These will be the corners of the bag. To attach the long sides

of the bag bottom to the main bag, pull the side of the bag into position to meet the bottom at the corner, then pin in place as shown. Pin carefully, easing in any extra fabric.

4) You will start stitching the long side of the bottom to the bag at the point where the short side stitching has ended (at the corner).

5) Repeat on the opposite side of the bag bottom. You will have a square bottom with very slightly rounded corners.

6

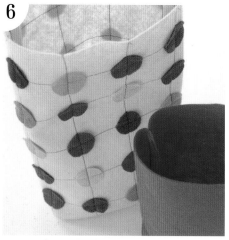

7

8

9

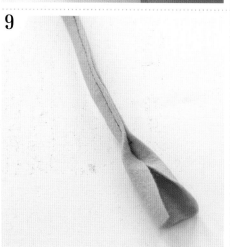

10

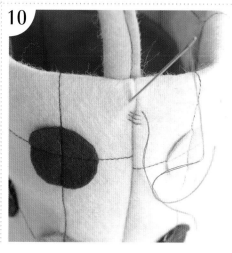

6) With your outer bag complete, it is time to make the lining. Repeat Steps 1–5, using the lining pieces. The lining will be several inches shorter than the outer bag.

7) Turn the outer bag inside out and the lining right side (p. 120) out. Place the lining inside the outer bag so that the right sides are together and pin the lining to the outer bag, matching up the top edges. Sew around the top perimeter of the bag, leaving a 3" (7.5 cm) gap for turning.

8) Turn the bag through the gap so the right sides are out. Tuck in the raw edges at the gap and handsew closed with a slip stitch (p. 121). Push the lining down into the bag until the bottoms touch each other. This

will fold down the top edge of the outer bag, forming a finished "cuff" that keeps the lining from showing.

9) Fold the long edges of the strap in, a little less than ½" (1.3 cm), until they almost meet in the center. Now fold in half along the center line so raw edges are tucked inside. Pin and stitch along the edge to close, about ⅛" (3 mm) from the edge.

10) Place about 1" (2.5 cm) of each end of the strap inside the bag at the side seams. With doubled thread, make multiple diagonal whipstitches (p. 121) to secure handle to bag. Alternatively, you can stitch the strap on with an "X" shape, going over it multiple times for strength.

swirl bag

To create the Swirl Bag, follow the instructions for the Dots Bag and use diagrams B and C on p. 110 for cutting dimensions; embellish the bag with swirls, instead of dots. When you reach Step 6, turn both the outer bag and the lining right side out, then put the lining inside the outer bag, with wrong sides together. Insert the ends of the 2 straps between the outer bag and the lining as shown in the photo at right, before pinning and then topstitching (p. 120) around the perimeter of the bag, following the top edge of the outer bag.

swirl bag

crosshatch PATCHWORK

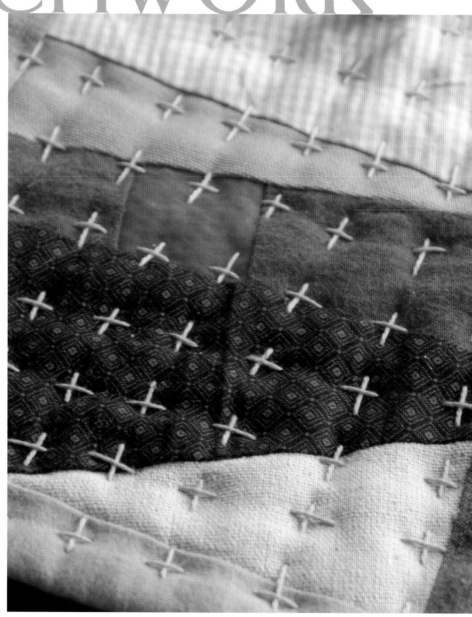

Patchwork is a perfect way to play with color and geometry; even first-timers can make something beautiful. But if you are looking to go beyond beauty and give your patchwork some texture, a bit of twinkle, and sense of humor, try this easy crosshatch stitch to cover the surface. The stitch is uncomplicated, almost childlike in its simplicity, yet it adds a modern twist and a quirky character to the traditional patchwork. Even better, it adds a deliciously nubby texture that is as appealing to the hands as it is to the eye.

¼ yd (23 cm) each of 5 or 6 plain cottons
(solids are best, but subtle pattern is okay)

½ yd (46 cm) of backing fabric
(I used red cotton)

¼ yd (23 cm) of fabric for the border
(I used natural linen and blue denim for
the pot holders shown here)

½ yd (46 cm) of cotton batting

embroidery floss

crosshatch patchwork panel
(and pot holder)

1) Begin with a blank sheet of paper and draw a box
the size of the pieced panel you need for your project
(for the pot holder, mine measured about 6 x 8" [15 x
20.5 cm]). Using a straightedge, draw in your pieced
design, using a few angled lines that stretch from one
side of the box to the other. Add other lines running
horizontally at various angles. Add one or two vertical
lines within the angled pieces (see diagram A above
right for an example). When you are happy with the
design, number each piece.

2) Trace the lines onto a piece of tracing paper and
cut them out along the lines to make templates. Be
sure to transfer the number for each piece to the
tissue paper.

3) Pin these tissue templates onto the various fabrics
and cut around them, leaving a seam allowance of ¼ "
(6 mm) on all sides (3a). Leave the numbered paper on
them so you can remake the puzzle and see how the
whole thing works (3b).

4) Start piecing up from the bottom of the design,
working in horizontal rows. Place 2 of the pieces
right sides (p. 120) together and pin. Sew the pieces
together. Always sew the vertical seams together first,
then the diagonal seams.

toolbox

paper, tracing paper, and pen or pencil

ruler or straightedge

embroidery needle

finished size

Linen-border pot holder: about 8 x 7½"
(20.5 x 19 cm)
Denim-border pot holder: about 8½ x 10"
(21.5 x 25.5 cm)

cut and stitch

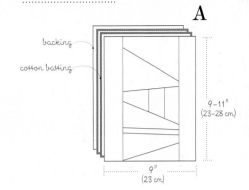

A

backing

cotton batting

9–11"
(23–28 cm)

9"
(23 cm)

handsew rows of running stitch (p. 121) at
½" (1.3 cm) intervals

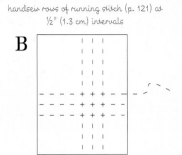

B

NOTE: All seam allowances are ¼" (6 mm) unless otherwise indicated.

1

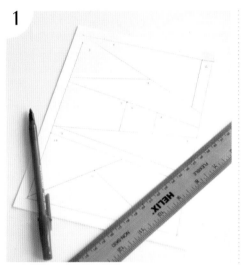

2

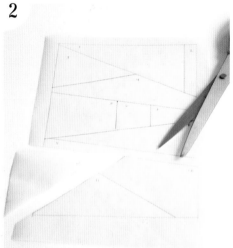

3a

3b

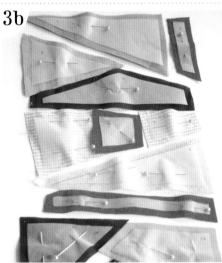

4

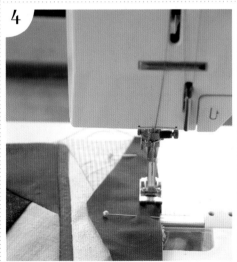

5

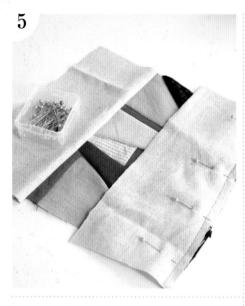

6

7

8

9

5) Iron your pieced panel flat and trim any excess fabric from the edges if necessary. It doesn't need to be square, but the edges should be even. If you would like your pot holder to be larger than the patchwork panel, add pieces of border fabric to create the desired finished size of your pot holder (my borders added just a few inches). The borders don't need to be symmetrical—one can be wider than the other or they can be angled, like mine were, to give the finished project a jaunty attitude.

6) Cut a piece of backing fabric, and 2 (or 3!) layers of cotton batting to the size of your finished front. Put the front and the back material together with right sides (p. 120) together. Add the layers of batting beneath the backing fabric. Pin and sew all the way around the perimeter, leaving open a 3" (7.5 cm) gap for turning. Trim the seams and clip the corners (clip triangles at the corners with the point of the triangle toward the seam, be careful not to clip through the seam!) to reduce bulk, then turn the pot holder right side out (see diagram A on p. 117). Tuck in the raw edges at the gaps and handstitch closed with a slip stitch (p. 121).

7) Iron the sewn pot holder flat.

8) Thread a large needle with embroidery floss. Starting about halfway down the pot holder, sew a row of running stitch (p. 121) from side to side (go through all layers). The stitches should be about ¼" (6 mm) long with a ¼" (6 mm) gap between each. Continue these horizontal rows of stitching, each about ½" (1.3 cm) apart, all the way up to the top of the pot holder, with the last row about ½" (1.3 cm) away from the edge.

9) Now turn the pot holder 90 degrees and begin sewing along the other axis (see diagram B on p. 117), crossing each existing stitch as you go to make a plus sign. Continue until the entire surface is covered with the little crosshatches.

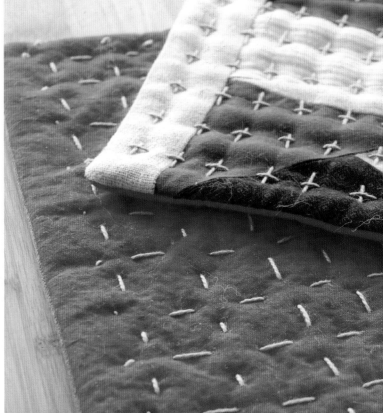

GLOSSARY OF TERMS

BASTE

Using long, loose stitches to hold something in place temporarily (similar to a running stitch but using longer stitches). You can baste by hand or machine (set the machine to the longest stitch length).

FRENCH SEAM

A seam that hides the raw edges by folding the seam allowance back onto itself, often used with delicate fabrics like silk charmeuse. To sew a French seam, lay the two pieces wrong sides together and sew the seam, using only $1/3$ of the seam allowance. Then turn the piece inside out and lay right sides together so that the seam is folded back onto itself. Sew the seam using the remaining $2/3$ of the seam allowance. The seam is now finished on both sides, with the raw edges encased inside the seam.

GUSSET

A small piece of fabric (often triangular, but can be other shapes as well) inserted between two main pieces of fabric to add space or reduce stress on a seam.

RIGHT SIDE

The right side of the fabric is the front side or the side that should be on the outside of a finished garment or project. On a printed fabric, the print will be stronger on the right side.

SEAM ALLOWANCE

The seam allowance is the amount of fabric that is between the raw edge and the seam.

SELVEDGE

The selvedges are the tightly woven borders on the lengthwise edges of the fabric.

TOPSTITCH

Stitching that shows on the right side (outside) of the garment or project. Topstitching is usually completed by stitching with the fabric right side up, often at a set distance from an edge.

WRONG SIDE

The wrong side of the fabric is the underside, or the side that should be on the inside of a finished garment. On a printed fabric, the print will be lighter or less obvious on the wrong side.

ZIGZAG STITCH

The zigzag stitch setting on your sewing machine creates a zigzagging stitch that is most often used to finish raw edges in order to prevent raveling. This can be used in lieu of a serger or pinking shears. If your fabric is very thin or delicate, it is usually best to finish both raw edges at a seam together, rather than separately.

TECHNIQUES GLOSSARY

OVERHAND KNOT

The overhand knot is the basic knot for tying off thread. Make a loop with the thread. Pass the thread that lies behind the loop over the front thread and through the loop. Pull tight.

RUNNING STITCH

Working from right to left, make a row of running stitch by bringing the needle up and insert at 1, bring up at 2 (about ⅛″ [3 mm] from 1, or as desired); repeat.

SLIP STITCH

Working from right to left, join two pieces of fabric by taking a ¼″ (6 mm) long stitch into the folded edge of one piece of fabric and bringing the needle out. Insert the needle into the folded edge of the other piece of fabric, directly across from the point where the thread emerged from the previous stitch. Repeat by inserting the needle into the first piece of fabric. The thread will be almost entirely hidden inside the folds of the fabric.

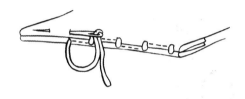

WHIPSTITCH

Bring the needle up at 1, insert at 2, and bring up at 3. These quick stitches do not have to be very tight or close together, unless you are whipstitching in place in a small area.

TEMPLATES

Here are the pattern pieces for the Top with a Border on p. 64. Photocopy the pattern at 300% enlargement for proper scale. You may need to piece the pattern together from more than one 8½ × 11" (20.5 × 28 cm) copy. Use the type printed on the pattern as a guide to realign the sections. Seam allowances are included in the pattern pieces. Be sure to place the designated pattern edge on the fabric fold.

½" seam allowance
included

SIZE SMALL

tank top
cut 1 front on fold
cut 1 back on fold

ENLARGE TO 300%

place on fold

½" seam allowance included

SIZE MEDIUM

tank top
front and back
cut 1 front on fold
cut 1 back on fold

place on fold

ENLARGE TO 300%

½" seam allowance included

SIZE LARGE

tank top
front and back
cut 1 front on fold
cut 1 back on fold

place on fold

ENLARGE TO 300%

RESOURCES

FABRICS

BRITEX FABRICS

146 Geary St., San Francisco, CA 94108

(415) 392-2910

This store is worth a pilgrimage to San Francisco for its four floors of the world's most beautiful fabric.

britexfabrics.com

ELFRIEDE'S FINE FABRICS

2425 Canyon Blvd., Boulder, CO 80302

(303) 447-0132

A local Colorado secret for extraordianary fabrics and one-of-a-kind notions of the highest quality. Every trip to Elfriede's is a journey of inspiration.

elfriedesfinefabrics.com

FABRIC.COM

Excellent selection of value-priced fabrics, including 54" (137 cm) wide douppioni silks in an array of colors, cotton duck, and linens in a dazzling variety of weights and colors.

fabric.com

HANCOCK FABRICS

Large selection of fabrics and notions with stores nationwide.

(877) FABRICS

hancockfabrics.com

HARTS FABRIC

Great online source for linen, cotton denim, and duck, plus a wide selection of eco-fiber blends.

hartsfabric.com

JO-ANN FABRICS AND CRAFTS

A large selection of fabrics and notions with stores nationwide.

(888) 739-4120

joann.com

VOGUE FABRICS STORE

An excellent online source for cottons, linens, silks, and sheers in a wide variety of fiber blends, weights, and colors.

voguefabricsstore.com

FELT

FELTORAMA

Great source for Eco Felt (made from recycled plastic bottles) in lots of colors.

(888) 393-4050

feltorama.com

FELTPRO

100% wool and wool/rayon felt in a wide array of colors and blends.

(479) 790-5079

feltpro.net

ERICA'S

100% wool and wool/rayon blend felt by the yard or the 12" (30.5 cm) square.

ericas.com

NOTIONS

M&J TRIMMINGS

New York-based notions superstore with buttons, ribbons, trims, buckles, and more.

mjtirms.com

CREATE FOR LESS

Online source for thousands of notions and sewing tools from pins to pressing tools to iron-on adhesives.

createforless.com

J CAROLINE CREATIVE

Wonderful selection of buckles and slides as well as lots of other appealing notions.

jcarolinecreative.com

PELLON STABILIZERS AND ADHESIVES

Pellon makes a large selection of stabilizers and fusible adhesives like Wonder-Under and Peltex.

shoppellon.com

MAGAZINES

STITCH MAGAZINE

Innovative and hip ideas for the modern stitcher from *Quilting Arts* and Interweave.

interweavestitch.com

THANKS My eternal gratitude goes to my amazing mother, Marlies Harris, for her unstinting supply of enthusiasm, optimism, and creative thinking. It is her unwavering support and you-can-do-anything! ethic that has gotten me over all the rough patches and treacherous tangles of my life. It was she who bought the fabric and the sewing machines all those years ago. It was she who stepped on the pins I dropped into the carpet, and it was she who allowed me to stay up into the wee hours of the morning, trying to conjure something from the ethers down to earth. This book is a tribute to her belief in magic and the magic of her belief.

Thanks to my family for their support and patience while I sewed right through dinner and took over the house for photo shoots. To Rainer for being one of my harshest yet wisest critics. To my beautiful Camille for being my model and muse.

Thanks always to my husband, Tom, for his steadiness, wisdom, and quirky inspiration.

Thanks to the wise and feisty Linda Ligon who first came up with the idea of a sewing book that begins by first making the fabric. To the graceful Elfriede Gamow who has inspired a generation of people to sew with her unerring style and unending technical prowess. To Julie Stutsman Garner, who was one of my earliest—and favorite—partners in crime. To Margaret Williman Blatter who showed me that you can climb mountains and make slippers on the very same day. To Pam Lemme, Nini Coleman, and Eliza Kuelthau for practicing random inspiration and selfless acts of "hipness." To Rachel Warwick, one of the quirkiest, smartest, and craftiest people I know. To Corinna Nolting, who knows the poetry of beautifully made things.

My humblest and most appreciative gratitude to all the tireless people at Interweave who cajoled and corrected but never coerced even as I stretched deadlines to their breaking point and sent out crabby e-mails at all hours of the night and day. I am especially grateful to Tricia Waddell who found time to be a patient and clever editor/collaborator even as her inbox overflowed with all her other dizzying responsibilities. To Katrina Loving for teasing out all the inconsistency and confusion and sculpting a cogent book, and to Kerry Jackson, Rebecca Campbell, Connie Poole, and Nancy Arndt for making it all come together beautifully in the end.